221.95
K12
a
　　Kamm, Josephine.
　　　　Kings, prophets, and
　history.

DATE | ISSUED

221.95
K12
a
　　Kamm, Josephine.
　　　　Kings, prophets, and
　history.

Temple Israel
Library
Minneapolis, Minn.

———

Please sign your full name on the above card.

Return books promptly to the Library or Temple Office.

Fines will be charged for overdue books or for damage or loss of same.

KINGS, PROPHETS AND HISTORY

A NEW LOOK AT THE OLD TESTAMENT

KINGS, PROPHETS AND HISTORY

A New Look at the Old Testament

by

JOSEPHINE KAMM

with illustrations by
GWYNETH COLE

McGRAW-HILL BOOK COMPANY
NEW YORK . SAN FRANCISCO
TORONTO

First publication in the United States
of America, 1966

© Josephine Kamm 1965

Library of Congress Catalog Card
Number: 66–16413

33260

First published under the title A NEW LOOK AT THE OLD
TESTAMENT, by Victor Gollancz Ltd., Great Britain.

Printed in Great Britain

For

Richard and Oliver

AUTHOR'S NOTE

I should like to thank Rabbi Dr. Leslie I. Edgar and Mr. Alan Millard for their kindness in reading this book in typescript and for many valuable suggestions. I should also like to thank Miss Marjorie Moos and my publisher, Miss Livia Gollancz, for their help and encouragement.

J. K.

CONTENTS

LIST OF ILLUSTRATIONS

I PLATES

II DRAWINGS

III MAPS

INTRODUCTION

FOUR THOUSAND YEARS is a long stretch of time, but we must look back along those years if we are to understand the real beginnings of Bible history.

But, first of all, what does the word "Bible" mean? It is a Greek word and it simply means "book". The Greeks wrote books on a fabric made from a plant called "Biblos", and they called their books "Bibloi" or "Biblia". To us, the Bible is very much more than just a book. It is *the* Book. It is not really one book at all, but a large number of short books. These books were written at different times and then collected together.

The Bible is divided into two parts, the Hebrew Bible (or Old Testament as it is usually called), and the New Testament. The Old Testament is, of course, much older than the New. It is the Bible of the Jews, who were known as Hebrews or Israelites in ancient times.

Some people believe that every word in the Bible is true. Other people think that parts of it are told in parables, that is to say, as stories which are meant to show the importance of being honest, just, kind, truthful, and so on. We may believe that every word is true; or we may think that parts are told in parables, and that therefore some of the stories did not happen exactly as they were written. Indeed, many of the events described in the Bible took place so very long ago that it is not possible to get at the absolute truth, especially when more than one account is given of the same event. But whatever we believe, one thing is absolutely certain. Through the ages very many people have been helped, comforted, and inspired by the Bible. It has taught them reverence for God, who created the world; and it has taught them the good qualities in life which really matter.

Most of the Old Testament was first written in Hebrew although some parts were written in Aramaic, a language which is very like Hebrew. The New Testament was written in Greek. The various books had to be translated before people who did not understand these ancient languages could read them.

In England, what is called the "Authorised Version" of the Bible in English was printed in 1611 in the reign of King James I. It is written in very beautiful language, but it is not always easy to understand. Indeed, the difficulty in translating from ancient languages often makes it impossible to give the exact meaning and so some of the sense is lost. Another English version—the "Revised Version"—was printed in 1885; but the Authorised Version has remained the most popular because of the beauty of its language and so I have used it here. Other English versions have been printed during the twentieth century, in England and in America. In England, the latest is an entirely fresh translation from the Greek of the New Testament, which was published in 1962. Scholars are also working on a fresh translation from the Hebrew of the Old Testament, but this will not be finished for some years.

This book is about the stories in the Hebrew Bible—the Old Testament. The Hebrew Bible was written by Jews, about Jews, and for Jews. It tells us something of their early history, and it is full of exciting tales. It was not written down from start to finish like an ordinary book, and the first parts are not always the oldest. In it, different ages are sometimes muddled together, and most of the books—as the various sections are called—have had bits added to them at different times. Yet, even though the Bible tells many different stories and covers a long distance of time, we can read it as one book. Each story reveals something fresh about the teachings of God; and, as the people grew more civilised, their ideas of what God demanded of them in their worship and their daily life became more advanced. The stories are all linked together by one theme—faith in God; and this theme, which runs right through the Bible, gives it its wonderful unity.

The Bible tells us a great deal about how people lived. There is something else which also helps us to understand them, and that is our growing knowledge of archaeology—the study of ancient things. Buried cities have been discovered, tombs have been opened; and the remains of such objects as pottery, bricks, jewellery, and writing tablets which have been dug up out of the ground help to show us what everyday life was like. All this makes the Bible stories seem much more real.

We now know that four thousand years ago, when there was no civilised life in England or America, there were people who could read and write. These people lived in Egypt and in the Empire of Babylonia, which stretched from the Persian Gulf through Asia to the Mediterranean Sea, and they lived there for a very long time. We know, too, that they built houses, monuments, and temples in honour of their gods. They worshipped many different gods and put images of them in their temples and their houses.

It is in Babylonia that our Bible story really starts. In—or near —the city of Ur, which at that time was the chief city, a child was born who, we are told, decided when he grew up that it was wrong to worship many gods. There was, he felt sure, only one God—the God of Righteousness. And so, because he felt that he could not worship his God in a place where everybody else— even his own father—worshipped many gods, he left his birth-place and went in search of a land where he could live and worship as he thought right and teach his faith to others. His name was Abraham; and his story, which happened nearly four thousand years ago, is told in the first chapter of this book.

CHAPTER I

ABRAHAM

IN ANCIENT TIMES the centre of the world as it was then known was in the region which today is called the Middle East. If you were to draw a line from Egypt up through Palestine (part of which is now the state of Israel) and Syria, and then down the River Euphrates to the Persian Gulf, you would have traced a wide semicircle. This semicircle—or crescent—was known as the Fertile Crescent because the land along it had plenty of water; and in the Middle East water has always been very important, for so much of the region is dry desert.

Many people lived in the Fertile Crescent; and wandering tribes from the desert used to visit it in search of water and pasture land for their cattle and flocks. But the region was not just the centre of the ancient world. It was also the centre of the religious history of the Jews.

Every religion tells a story about the creation of the world. "In the beginning", says the Hebrew Bible, "God created the heaven and the earth." The earth was empty and dark; "And God said, Let there be light: and there was light." And God divided light from darkness and so made day and night. Then when He had

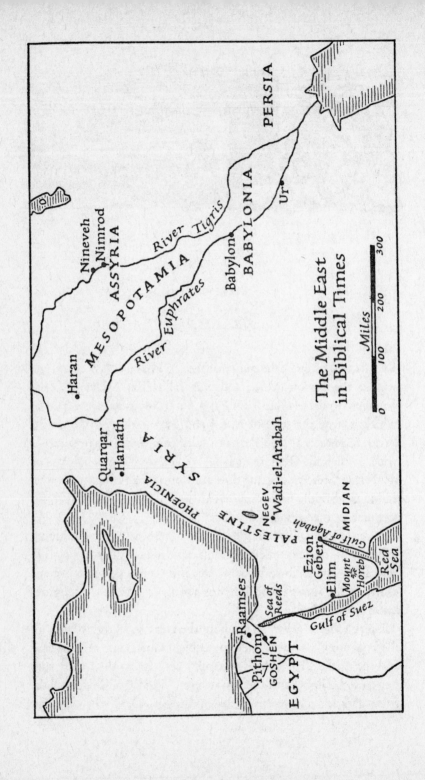

The Middle East in Biblical Times

made the different seasons and given shape to the world He created living animals, and finally He made man.

The Bible goes on to tell of Adam and his wife Eve, the first man and woman; of their children and their descendants. The writers of this story thought mistakenly that by God's command the people were drowned in a great flood of water as a punishment for their wicked ways. The people of those days did not understand that disasters such as floods and earthquakes take place naturally. They thought that when things went wrong they were being made to suffer for their wickedness. According to the Bible story, at the time of the great flood there was only one righteous man in the world. His name was Noah, and because he was a good man he and his family were saved from drowning. Noah, so the story goes, built a large wooden ark—or boat—in which he and his family and various animals and birds took shelter. The wooden ark floated safely on the flood waters until they died down; and so the earth was peopled again by Noah's descendants.

The story of the flood as it is told in the Hebrew Bible is very well known; but a number of other stories have been handed down to us about terrible floods which occurred in ancient times, and in Babylonian records there are references to a particularly bad one. These stories were not about Noah, but most of them relate that although many people were drowned a few were saved. And then, not so long ago, it was discovered that there certainly had been a very bad flood in the Middle East in very early days. In 1922 Sir Leonard Woolley, a British archaeologist, went out to the area to start, and take charge of, a series of excavations. Woolley studied the pottery and other objects which were being dug up in the soil of what had once been the city of Ur, an important centre of Babylonian civilisation. Ur was near the Persian Gulf at the south-eastern tip of the Fertile Crescent. The workmen who were doing the actual digging found a great deal of pottery and other objects, and these proved that people had once lived on the spot. But at a certain level as they dug downwards the soil changed to thick, clean clay, and there were no objects at all in the clay. The workmen dug eight feet down through the clay, and then they suddenly came upon a great many more objects—stone tools and hand-painted pottery. Woolley was certain from this discovery that the people who had used the stone tools and the pottery had been drowned in deep flood water which must have covered a large part of the city and had left behind it this thick deposit of clay; and years later, he concluded, other people had made their homes on top of the clay. Woolley's discovery suggests to us that the Bible and the Babylonian records refer to this special disaster.

And so we can see that even if the story of Noah did not happen exactly as the Bible tells us, the fact that there was one flood more terrible than the others is probably true. Men thought that the people who were drowned were being punished; and so the story of Noah was probably a parable told to try and persuade people to live better lives.

From their excavations—or digging operations—at Ur, Sir Leonard Woolley and other archaeologists have given us a clear idea of how the people actually lived four thousand years ago. Ur itself was surrounded by walls to protect it from attack by warlike enemy tribes. Within the walls there was a sacred area in which temples and shrines had been built in honour of the moon-god Nannar, whom the people worshipped. Although they worshipped many other gods, Nannar was the special god of Ur. To the west of the sacred area there was a high platform on which an immensely tall brick tower had been erected. Around the outside of the tower which was called the Ziggurat (ziggurat means pinnacle or mountain top) there were long winding stair-cases; and on the feast days of the moon-god, whose shrine stood on top of the tower, long religious processions passed up and down the stairs.

The district in which the people lived was outside the sacred area. There, the archaeologists found the remains of large brick houses, two stories high, some of them with as many as thirteen or fourteen rooms. In a book which Sir Leonard Woolley wrote about his discoveries, *Ur of the Chaldees*, there is a picture of one of the houses. It shows an inner courtyard with a tiled pavement on which stand two tall pottery jars. Doors lead off the courtyard, and tiled steps lead to the upper story, which has a wooden railing running round it. The courtyard is open to the sky, but the rooms on the upper story are covered with a flat roof on which the family who owned the house must often have sat in the cool of the evening. From the roof they could look down on other houses and large and beautiful gardens. They could also see beyond the city walls as far as the River Euphrates and the fields and pasture lands watered by canals which they had dug themselves.

The ordinary people of Ur used plain clay cooking pots and bowls; but some of the pottery found in the larger houses was decorated with lovely designs, and there were also vases and drinking cups for the more important people made of gold and silver, rich jewellery for the women, and weapons of war for the men.

The children of Ur went to school. We know this because clay tablets were found scratched with children's writing. These tablets showed that the children learned arithmetic and geometry, and also studied hymns which were sung to the various gods. The people made idols—or images—of their gods out of gold and silver, stone, wood and clay. Every house had its own little chapel in which stood a stone altar and images of the gods which the people worshipped. The priests honoured the kings of Ur as though they were gods instead of men. When a king died almost all his slaves drank poison in order that they should be buried with him in his tomb and so be able to accompany him to the after-life. People believed that they would live in the after-life as they had lived on earth and would need all the things they had formerly owned. This was the reason for such an apparently cruel and savage practice.

Sir Leonard Woolley called the picture in his book "a house of the time of Abraham" (see p. 37). He felt sure that he had discovered the very city in which the first Jewish hero was born, for the Bible mentions Ur of the Chaldees as Abraham's birthplace.

Abraham's father was called Terah. There is a story that Terah owned a shop in which he made idols and sold them for a living. This may not be true; but the Bible tells us that Terah worshipped idols, and he brought up his children to share his beliefs.

Many stories have been told which are not in the Bible about Terah and his idols, and very many more about Abraham. These stories—or legends as they are called—were related to the people of old by the Jewish rabbis—or teachers. The legends were not supposed to be true; but they were told by men who loved the Hebrew Bible and its heroes and were never tired of inventing stories about them.

One of these legends tells how Nimrod, king of Ur, who was worshipped as a god by his people, dreamed one night that a boy-child would soon be born who would prove that the king was not a god at all but just an ordinary man. The dream angered Nimrod so much that he gave orders that every boy born in Ur after that date should be killed at birth. The people, who had been taught to believe that the king could do no wrong, obeyed Nimrod's cruel command, all of them except one, the wife of Terah, the idol-maker. Terah's wife gave birth to a baby boy while her husband was away from home. She could not bear the thought that her child should be killed, and so she hid him in a cave and told nobody what she had done. She dared not visit the baby, and he would certainly have starved to death if God had not sent an angel to feed him. And, even more wonderful to relate, in the short space of twenty days the baby grew into a strong and healthy boy, who could walk and talk and praise God for saving his life. At first his parents could not believe that the boy was Abraham, their baby son; but when he had managed to convince them that he was, they rejoiced with him.

The rabbis who were fond of telling this story did not, of course, believe that it had actually happened or that the child had been fed by an angel. Abraham grew up at the same rate as any other child. They told the story to prove that Abraham, the first man to seek the one true God, had shown that Nimrod and the other kings of Ur were not gods but ordinary men.

The Bible does not tell us exactly how this change in Abraham came about. We can guess that even when he was young he could not believe that an idol made by a man could have any life or power of its own; and that as he looked about the world in which he lived he realised that some Being greater than man had made it and should be worshipped by everybody. It probably took Abraham many years to work out in his own mind that this being was the one God. When he had come to this conclusion he felt that he could no longer live in Ur, with its cruel religious practices; and so he decided to go right away. According to the Bible: "Now the Lord had said unto Abraham, Get thee out of thy country, and from thy kindred, and from thy father's house, unto a land that I will shew thee: And I will make of thee a great nation, and I will bless thee, and make thy name great; and thou shalt be a blessing. . .; and in thee shall all families of the earth be blessed."

Terah decided to leave Ur at the same time as his son. We do not know exactly why. It may simply have been that he did not want to part with his son. It may have been because of floods, famine or disease, or because he thought that Ur might be attacked and conquered by neighbouring tribes. All we do know from the Bible is that Terah with the rest of the family, his servants and slaves, and all the cattle he possessed went with Abraham on the first part of Abraham's journey. They journeyed northwards to Haran in Mesopotamia—the land between the two rivers, the Euphrates and the Tigris—which is now Iraq. The journey must have been slow and hard; for the travellers had to cross vast stretches of dry burning desert; and each night before they could pitch their goatskin tents they had to find a water-hole or an oasis —one of the rare spots which provided water and a little pasture for the animals.

Terah, who was worn out by his travels, decided to settle in

Haran. But Abraham soon set off again, taking with him his wife, Sarah, and his nephew, Lot, for he had no children of his own.

In those days a man's wealth was measured not in money but in animals; and Abraham, who possessed large herds of cattle and flocks of sheep and goats, must have been a rich man. He employed servants and herdsmen to look after the beasts; and as he journeyed he was joined by other travellers, who looked on him as the head man—or chief—of the tribe. It was a wandering tribe, living in tents and not in houses, and, led by Abraham, it journeyed slowly south-eastwards towards Palestine, the land of Canaan, as the Bible calls it.

Abraham's was one of a number of wandering tribes. Some of the wanderers never stayed in one place for more than a night or two; but others gave up their restless life and settled down to become workers or slaves in the homes of rich men. These people were given the name of "Habiru" (or "Apiru"). The word "Habiru" sounds very like the word "Hebrew"; and, as Abraham was the first person in the Bible to be called by the name of Hebrew, there may have been some connection between the Habiru and the Hebrews, as Abraham's people were called.

The land of Canaan was a small country, only about the size of Wales, but it had plenty of good pasture. The people were called Canaanites (Canaanite means merchant), but they were not, as Abraham soon found, very different from the people of Ur. In the countryside the shepherds and peasants worked hard from morning to night; but in the cities wealthy merchants and their families lived easy, comfortable lives. To Abraham's great grief, he also found that the Canaanites, like the people of Ur, worshipped idols, although they gave their idols different names. And they offered human beings as sacrifice to their gods.

The Hebrews copied the custom of sacrifice from their neighbours; but the sacrifices which they made to Abraham's God, who became their God also, were not of living men but of corn, oil and fruit, and sometimes of animals. The idea of sacrifice is to offer to the gods (or in the case of the Hebrews to God) something of real value, something which will be missed. The Hebrews, like the Canaanites, had slaves, for slavery was the usual practice of the day. The Canaanites often offered their slaves as sacrifices; but Abraham saw to it that *his* slaves were never cruelly treated or overworked. He was wise, thoughtful and extremely kind; and his servants and slaves looked on him more as a father than a master.

Abraham was also very generous. Once, the Bible tells us, he camped at a place which did not provide enough grazing land for all his flocks and for those of his nephew Lot. As Abraham was the elder and the head of the tribe he had every right to take the best land for himself. Instead, he turned to his nephew with these words: "Let there be no strife, I pray thee, between me and thee, and between my herdmen and thy herdmen; for we be brethren. Is not the whole land before thee? Separate thyself, I pray thee, from me; if thou wilt take the left hand, then I will go to the right; or if thou depart to the right hand, then I will go to the left."

And Lot, who had been invited by his uncle to take for himself the land he thought best, chose to go southwards along the valley of the River Jordan towards a city state in the plains called Sodom. Neither he nor Abraham knew at the time that the king of Sodom was on the point of going to war with the kings of several neighbouring city states. Lot had scarcely settled down when war broke out, and he and a number of the chief men of Sodom were taken prisoner by the other kings.

When Abraham heard that Lot was a prisoner he made up his mind to rescue him. The victorious kings, their armies and their captives had crossed the River Jordan and were making their way homewards; and Abraham, who had trained and armed his followers, crossed the river in pursuit. During the daytime Abraham's small army watched the slowly-moving procession from the shelter of a hide out; but at night they moved forward swiftly and silently. Then, when they had almost caught up with the victorious kings, Abraham's men were divided into three

companies. During the night while the enemy lay sleeping
Abraham sent one company to approach their tents from the
south, and ordered the others to attack the camp, one from the
east and one from the west. The battle which followed was very
short. The enemy were too confused and sleepy to make any
resistance, and Abraham's army rescued Lot and the other
prisoners and also captured a great deal of valuable booty. One
of the freed prisoners, a city ruler, was so grateful to Abraham
that he begged him to keep all the booty. But Abraham refused.
He had only done his duty, he said, and he wanted no reward.
"I have lift up mine hand unto the Lord, the most high God, the
possessor of heaven and earth, that I will not take from a thread
even to a shoe-latchet, and that I will not take anything that is
thine."

Abraham, who loved peace and hated war, was glad when he
did not have to fight any more. He liked best to sit at the entrance
to his tent in the evening when the day's work was done; and if
any strangers passed by his camp he would invite them in. Then
Sarah would prepare food for them, and Abraham and his guests
would talk together for hours on end. One of these guests, so the
Bible says, was sent by God to tell Abraham that he and Sarah
would have a son. Many years before God had promised Abraham, "I will make of thee a great nation." That meant that
Abraham would have many descendants; yet how could this
happen when he had no children? By this time Abraham and
Sarah were no longer young; and while the new promise gave
Abraham hope, Sarah feared that she was far too old to have a
child.

As time went on and still no son was born to him, Abraham
began to think that the promise might have meant something
different. Perhaps God meant him to choose some man to be his
son and heir, and, since he had no son of his own, this man would
inherit all his possessions and become the leader of the tribe when
he died. He decided that the best man he could choose would be
Eliezer, a man who had served him faithfully since he was a boy

and was by now the head of his household. But, the Bible tells us, the word of God came to Abraham telling him that his own son, and not Eliezer, should be his heir. And God ordered Abraham to look upwards at the night sky and try to count the stars, for his descendants would be as numerous as the stars. And Abraham "believed in the Lord; and he [God] counted it to him for righteousness".

Abraham did not, therefore, choose Eliezer as his heir, but by this time he was so sure that Sarah could never have a child that he decided to marry a second wife. In those days it was a very usual custom for a man to have more than one wife, and so Abraham's decision would not have been considered at all wrong or even strange. Indeed, according to the Bible, Sarah herself chose the woman. She "took Hagar her maid the Egyptian, . . . and gave her to her husband Abraham to be his wife". Sarah was still Abraham's chief wife, the most respected woman in the tribe. She was childless, but Abraham and Hagar had a son whom they named Ishmael.

And then, when Sarah had absolutely given up hope, she also gave birth to a son, who was called Isaac. The Bible says that God promised Abraham that Isaac, who in spite of the fact that he was the younger son should be his heir, and would be the father of one great nation and that Ishmael would be the father of another nation. Isaac's birth was a great joy to his parents; but unfortunately Sarah became jealous of Ishmael; and in the end she persuaded Abraham to disown him and to drive the boy and his mother out of the camp. Sarah's jealousy showed that she was not perfect; and Abraham was weak, for he could have refused to send Hagar and her little son away. But the men who wrote the Hebrew Bible never pretended that their heroes could do no wrong. The men and women in the Bible, even the greatest of them, acted like real people, and so they seem to us much more human and interesting than they would have done if they had been perfect.

Apart from her outburst of jealousy against Hagar and Ishmael,

Sarah was known to be kind and generous. The name Sarah means "princess"; and throughout her life, so one of the old legends goes, there were three signs which proved that she was good and noble. The first sign was that the flaps of her tent were always open, as an invitation to strangers to share the food she prepared for her husband and son. The second was that a light burned inside the tent day and night. No human being had kindled the light, and it never went out. The third sign was a cloud which hung over the entrance to the tent and sheltered everybody inside from the burning sun. The heavenly light and the sheltering cloud meant, according to the legend, that Sarah was eager to protect all people in need of help. When she died the light went out; the tent flaps closed and could not be opened; and the cloud vanished into the sky.

Both Abraham and Sarah loved their fellow people. They were made most unhappy by a sudden disaster which destroyed two small city states near the Dead Sea: Sodom, where Abraham's nephew Lot and his family lived, and the neighbouring state of Gomorrah. The destruction was probably caused by a violent earthquake, which buried the houses and all the people in them. Abraham did not realise this. Like everybody else, he was certain that God had decided to punish the people of Sodom and Gomorrah, who were well known to lead very evil lives. According to the Bible, God told Abraham that He intended to destroy the cities; and Abraham implored God to spare them for the sake of the few righteous people who lived there. But, sad to say, there were no righteous people at all except Lot. God was willing to spare Lot, who was ordered to flee with his wife and two daughters before disaster overtook his home. They were to travel as fast as they could and not look back; but it is said that while Lot and his daughters obeyed their orders, Lot's wife turned to see what was happening and was immediately changed into a pillar of salt for her disobedience. This story probably means that Lot and his family escaped only just in time and that, by hesitating even for a minute, Lot's wife was overwhelmed by the earthquake. It is interesting, too, to know that to the west of the southern shores of the Dead Sea there is a range of small hills many of which are made of rock salt. Blocks of salt from these hills have been worn away by the weather and washed downhill by heavy rains. Some of them look strangely like statues; and so it is easy to see how a story like the story of Lot's wife came about.

The disaster made Abraham desperately unhappy but it did not weaken his faith in God. And then, as the Bible tells it, his belief that whatever God demanded must somehow be right was put to a most terrible test: Abraham seemed to hear the voice of God commanding him to kill his own son. "Take now thy son, thine only son Isaac, whom thou lovest, and get thee into the land of Moriah; and offer him there for a burnt offering upon one of the mountains which I will tell thee of."

Today, we cannot for a moment imagine that God could ever have demanded such a cruel test of Abraham's faith. But whoever wrote this story as it appears in the Bible wanted to teach two things. The first was that a really religious person must be ready to do God's will however hard it may be. The second was that God Himself condemned the practice of human sacrifice. When we read the story today we have to remember that to Abraham— and even to the writer—the test would not have seemed so cruel and senseless as it does to us. As we know, it was the custom in those days for pagan people to sacrifice to their gods the things they treasured most, and it was not unusual for them to offer up their own children in this way. And so we are told that Abraham, who must have thought that he should be ready to offer to his God the thing he loved above all else on earth, made ready to do this dreadful deed. He took Isaac to a remote place in the mountains. There he built an altar and piled wood on it; and he bound the boy with ropes and lifted him on to the wood. Then he took a knife in his hand and was just about to strike his son dead and burn his body on the altar when a voice ordered him to stop. The voice told Abraham that he had proved his faith and that God did not wish him to harm Isaac in any way. And Abraham,

after releasing his son, took a ram which had been caught by
its horns in a nearby thicket and offered the animal as a sacrifice
to God in place of Isaac.

At that time the sacrifice of animals was not considered wrong;
but later writers in the Hebrew Bible realised that God, who
forbade human sacrifice, did not want the sacrifice of animals
either and that this practice also should be stopped. To the
Hebrews of Abraham's day, however, only the sacrifice of human
beings was forbidden.

As Abraham grew older and knew that he had not much longer
to live, he began to be troubled by the question of Isaac's future.
Sarah was now dead; and if Isaac married a Canaanite woman he
might forget about the worship of God and, instead, follow the
practices of the people of the country. Abraham therefore asked
the faithful Eliezer to travel back to Haran in Mesopotamia,
where some of the family still lived, and to choose a wife for
Isaac from among them.

Eliezer did as he was asked. He gladly undertook the long
journey; and before he entered the city of Haran he stopped to
rest for a while near a well from which the women came to draw
water every evening. As he rested a beautiful young woman
approached, carrying an earthenware pitcher. When she saw a
stranger seated near the well she asked him if he would like a
drink. He thanked her and said he would; and the young woman
drew water for Eliezer and also for his camels.

Eliezer then asked the young woman her name, and she told
him that she was Rebekah, the daughter of one of Abraham's
brothers. Eliezer decided at once that, since Rebekah was kind as
well as beautiful, he would ask her to return with him to Canaan
to become the wife of her cousin, Isaac. Rebekah agreed, and her
father gave his consent. When she and Isaac met they fell in love
with one another and became man and wife. According to one
of the old legends, when Isaac first saw Rebekah he knew that he
had found a woman worthy to take his mother's place in the
tribe. And so he led Rebekah towards Sarah's tent, which had

remained closed and dark ever since her death. When Rebekah touched the tent flaps they parted as though by magic. As she crossed the threshold the tent was suddenly filled with the eternal light; and above the entrance the sheltering cloud formed once more.

Abraham's work was now done; and he "died in a good old age, an old man, and full of years; and was gathered to his people". And his two sons, Isaac his son and heir, and Ishmael, the son of Hagar whom he had disowned, buried him in the cave where Sarah's body already lay buried, on a strip of land which Abraham had bought and set aside for the purpose.

And because he was the first man to break away from the pagan customs and beliefs of his world, all the millions of people who believe in the One God today can look back on him as their father Abraham.

CHAPTER II

ISAAC, JACOB AND JOSEPH

IT VERY OFTEN happens that the children of a really great man grow up without their father's fine character, and this is certainly true of Isaac, Abraham's dearly loved son. The Bible does not tell us very much about Isaac, but it is clear that he was a kindly man and a lover of peace, although he was too easy-going to make a real leader. His love of peace was his best quality, and he showed it at a time when fighting was constantly breaking out between the Canaanite tribes and those of neighbouring countries.

Once during a period of famine, when all the crops had failed after a bad drought, Isaac and his herdsmen went in search of pasture and water for the cattle. They drove the herds into the valley of Gerar near the land called the Negeb ("Negeb" means "the south country") in which a warlike people, the Philistines, were living. Isaac's father had camped there before him, and Abraham's servants had dug wells of clear water, which in the years that followed had become choked with drifting desert sand. When Isaac had found places where wells had been dug his servants began to clear the sand from the first one and soon, says the Bible, "found there a well of springing water". But some

Philistine herdsmen, who had seen what was happening, quarrelled with Isaac's herdsmen, saying, "The water is ours". Isaac had no intention of letting the quarrel develop into a fight, and so he ordered his servants to leave the well to the Philistines and dig one of the other wells. This they did, but the Philistines claimed the second well too. Once again Isaac ordered his servants to dig elsewhere, and they found a third well. This time the Philistines did not disturb them; and Isaac called the well "Rehoboth" (which means "room" or "broad places"), saying, "For now the Lord hath made room for us, and we shall be fruitful in the land."

In modern times the Negeb (or the Negev as it is usually called) has been very much in the news. For more than a thousand years it had been dry and stony, and very few people had been able to keep cattle or grow crops there. Abraham's wells had long since been forgotten, and because the water under the soil was undrinkable most people thought that the Negev could never be cultivated. In 1947, however, a Jewish state—the state of Israel—was created, of which the Negev formed a part. In the nearby valley of Gerar the Israelis, as the people of Israel are called, discovered some very ancient, disused wells which were buried in sand and rubble. They began to clear away the rubbish and dig; and, like the servants of Abraham and Isaac before them, they came on clear, springing water.

According to the Bible, God appeared to Isaac in the night, saying, "I am the God of Abraham thy father; fear not, for I am with thee and will bless thee, and multiply thy seed for my servant Abraham's sake."

It seemed right to Isaac to stay near the spot where he believed he had heard the voice of God. He built an altar there and worshipped God, and settled down to live. His servants dug another well; and as his herds and flocks of animals prospered, in time he became rich and important. In fact, he became so important that Abimelech, the Philistine chief, decided that he had better make friends with him. And Isaac, instead of reminding Abimelech of how unkindly his servants had once behaved, ordered a special feast to be prepared. When he and Abimelech had eaten they swore that they and their servants would live together in peace. That same day the well which Isaac's servants had dug was named "Shibah" (which means "swearing"). In later days a city was built near the ancient well, and the city was called "Beer-sheba" (which means the "well of the oath" or "well of swearing").

At this spot Abraham had once pitched his tents, and he had planted a tamarisk tree in Beer-sheba, and "sojourned in the Philistines' land many days". Planting a tamarisk was a wise thing to do, for the tamarisk is one of the few trees which will grow in such a dry country as the Negev. When the Israelis began to cultivate the Negev, as they are now doing, they planted as many as 2,000,000 tamarisk seedlings, which took root and soon began to flourish.

The Bible stories about Isaac's love of peace show him in a good light; but the other stories about him are not so pleasant, for they show how he caused trouble in his own family. He and his wife, Rebekah, had twin sons. The elder twin, a strong and ruddy-looking boy with a thick mat of hair, was named Esau; and the younger, who was smaller, was called Jacob. The story goes that Esau was the elder by only a few minutes, and that Jacob was born grasping his brother by the heel, as though he had been doing his best to be born first, and the name "Jacob" actually means "he takes by the heel", or "supplants" (that is to say, over-throws).

Isaac and Rebekah were proud of their sons, but they did not love them equally. Isaac favoured Esau, who grew into a wild, bold man, and a clever hunter of deer and other game. The Bible says that "Isaac loved Esau, because he did eat of his venison". Isaac was certainly rather greedy, and looked forward to eating the fresh meat which Esau brought back with him from his hunting expeditions. But he probably also admired Esau for his skill and energy and loved him for his high spirits and his boldness.

Rebekah, on the other hand, much preferred Jacob, who became a quiet and thoughtful man, always ready to listen to her advice. Rebekah believed (probably because she wanted so much to believe it) that God's promise to multiply the descendants of Isaac would be fulfilled through Jacob and not through his elder brother. And in after years the Hebrews always thought that they were descended from Jacob, and that the descendants of Esau were the Edomites, who belonged to another tribe.

Because Isaac made a favourite of Esau and Rebekah always took Jacob's part, the brothers became jealous of one another, and there was no real peace in the family. Rebekah must often have told Jacob that God intended him to be the real heir and the head of the tribe; and there are two Bible stories which show how Jacob himself tried to make this come true. In both stories he treated his brother very badly.

The first story relates that one day Esau returned home worn out and hungry after a day's hunting to find his younger brother making a thick pottage—or soup—of red lentils. "And Esau said to Jacob, Feed me, I pray thee, with that same red pottage; for I am faint . . . And Jacob said, Sell me this day thy birthright."

Now the birthright, which Esau gave away so carelessly, was the right of the first-born son to inherit his father's property. But the birthright meant something more than that. It meant that when a man died his first-born—or eldest—son inherited also the responsibility for caring for his family and for keeping alive their faith in God. Esau was not the sort of man to take these responsibilities at all seriously. "I am at the point to die [of hunger]", he said, "of what profit shall this birthright do to me? And Jacob said, Swear to me this day; and he sware unto him: and he sold his birthright unto Jacob. Then Jacob gave Esau bread and pottage of lentils; and he did eat and drink, and rose up, and went his way: thus Esau despised his birthright."

Esau bothered very little about his family's faith in God. Indeed, he married two pagan women who belonged to the tribe of the Hittites, one of the most powerful tribes in the country, who never

B

learned to worship the one God. And yet, although Esau "despised"—or cared nothing for—his birthright, there is no excuse for Jacob who tricked him out of it, in spite of the fact that Jacob took his family responsibilities very seriously indeed.

In the second of the two Bible stories Jacob played an even meaner trick on his brother. By this time Isaac was an old man and completely blind. One day he sent for his elder son, and said to him: "Behold now, I am old, I know not the day of my death: Now therefore take, I pray thee, thy weapons, thy quiver and thy bow, and go out to the field, and take me some venison; and make me savoury meat, such as I love, and bring it to me, that I may eat; that my soul may bless thee before I die."

In this story, Isaac could not have known that Esau had thought so little of his birthright that he had exchanged it for a dish of pottage; for if he had known he would not have offered to give Esau the special blessing given by a man only to his eldest son and heir.

Esau, who did not tell him what he had done, went off on his hunting expedition. Meanwhile, Rebekah, who had overheard all that had been said, made up her mind that Jacob should have the blessing instead of Esau. She therefore told him to bring her two kids from the flock so that she could cook them in the way her husband liked best. When she had done this, she said, Jacob could take the dish to his father and receive his blessing. But even though Isaac was blind, Jacob objected, he could easily tell the difference between his sons. If Isaac touched his hand he would know; for Jacob's hands and arms were smooth but Esau's were covered with thick hair. "My father, peradventure,* will feel me", he went on, "and I shall seem to him as a deceiver; and I shall bring a curse upon me, and not a blessing. And his mother said unto him, Upon me be thy curse, my son; only obey my voice, and go fetch me them."

So Jacob, who wanted the blessing badly, did as his mother told him. When the kids had been killed and cooked Rebekah

* Perhaps.

gave Jacob some of Esau's clothes to wear, and she draped the skins of the kids over his hands, arms and neck, so that they should feel hairy and rough and Isaac should be deceived into thinking that he was really Esau.

Isaac was very suspicious when Jacob entered his tent, saying, "I am Esau, thy firstborn. I have done according as thou badest me: arise, I pray thee, sit and eat of my venison, that thy soul may bless me." It seemed to Isaac that the food had been brought to him far too soon, for Esau's hunting expeditions generally took a whole day or longer. So he said to Jacob, "Come near, I pray thee, that I may feel thee, my son, whether thou be my very son Esau or not. And Jacob went near unto Isaac his father; and he felt him, and said, The voice is Jacob's voice, but the hands are the hands of Esau. And he discerned him not, because his hands were hairy, as his brother Esau's hands." Isaac therefore ate the food, and when he had eaten he blessed Jacob as he should have blessed only his eldest son: "Therefore God give thee of the dew of heaven, and the fatness of the earth, and plenty of corn and wine: Let people serve thee, and nations bow down to thee. Be lord over thy brethren, and let thy mother's sons bow down to thee: cursed be every one that curseth thee, and blessed be he that blesseth thee."

Jacob had scarcely departed when Esau entered his father's tent, hot and weary from the chase. As soon as Isaac heard Esau's voice he realised that he had been tricked; but when Esau asked his father to bless him Isaac had to explain that he had already given the blessing to Jacob. Naturally, Esau was furiously angry and he told Isaac how Jacob had tricked him twice. He implored his father to bless him, too; but Isaac could not take back what had been said. In his blessing he had asked God to make Jacob lord —or chief—of the tribe, and although Jacob had misled him, he knew that he would make a better leader than his elder brother. And so he said sadly to Esau: "What shall I do now unto thee, my son? And Esau said to his father, Hast thou but one blessing, my father? Bless me, even me also, O my father. And Esau lifted up his voice and wept. And Isaac his father answered and said unto him, Behold, thy dwelling shall be the fatness of the earth, and of the dew of heaven from above; And by thy sword shalt thou live, and shalt serve thy brother; and it shall come to pass when thou shalt have the dominion, that thou shalt break his yoke from off thy neck."

Isaac must have realised that there would not be room in the same camp for Esau and the brother who had wronged him. But it was no comfort to Esau to learn that he must live far from his home; and he was so furious with Jacob that he plotted to kill him. Then Rebekah, who had been warned of the plot, advised Jacob to go into hiding until Esau's rage had died down. "Now therefore, my son . . ., arise, flee thou to Laban my brother to Haran; And tarry with him a few days, until thy brother's fury turn away . . .: then I will send, and fetch thee from thence: why should I be deprived also of you both in one day?"

In the Bible there are two versions to explain the reason for Jacob's flight. The second version tells us that Jacob left home for a very different reason. According to this story, Isaac and Rebekah had been deeply hurt by the behaviour of Esau's two pagan wives, who were a bad influence on their husband; and they wanted Jacob to do as Isaac had done before him and choose a wife from his own family. Jacob was therefore to go to Haran in search of a wife who, if she had not been brought up to worship God, would soon learn to do so. Before Jacob left home his father blessed him once more: "And God Almighty bless thee and make thee fruitful, and multiply thee, that thou mayest be a multitude of people; And give thee the blessing of Abraham, to thee, and to thy seed with thee; that thou mayest inherit the land wherein thou art a stranger, which God gave unto Abraham."

This version of the story makes it quite clear that Isaac thought Jacob would make a far better leader than Esau. The Bible does not say which of the two versions is the right one. The same thing happens quite often in the other books of the Bible; and so it may well be that when two versions of the same story are given, they

Reconstruction drawing of the Ziggurat at Ur (*courtesy British Museum*)

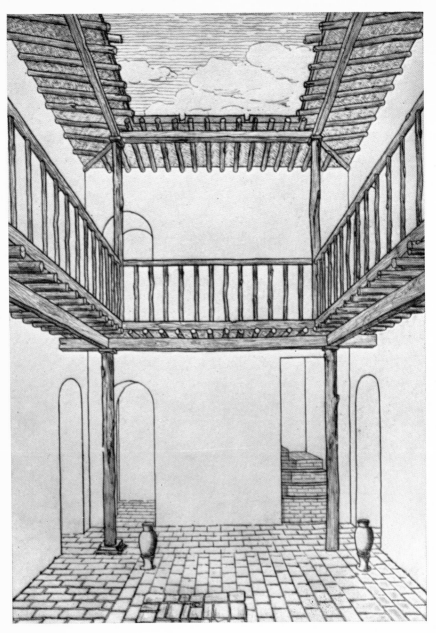

Reconstruction drawing of a house lived in at the time of Abraham
(*courtesy British Museum*)

are meant as parables and not as actual happenings. In the second version of this story of Jacob it may be that we are meant to believe that, although Jacob and his mother acted very wrongly, God had seen in Jacob the real leader of his people.

Both versions relate that Jacob left his home and went on a long journey. The Bible then goes on to tell us that while he was on his way to Haran Jacob dreamed one night of an immensely tall ladder reaching from the earth to the sky. In his dream he saw angels of God climbing up and down the ladder, and heard God's voice repeating the promise already made to Abraham and Isaac, that their descendants would multiply and spread over all the earth. To Jacob, the most surprising thing about the dream was not that he should think that he heard the voice of God, but that he should hear it far away from his home. Until that time he had imagined that God would only make His presence known in one particular place. He had not really understood that the God of Abraham and Isaac was the God of the whole world.

The morning after his strange dream Jacob went on his way again. When at last he reached Haran he discovered that his mother's brother, his uncle Laban, had two daughters, Leah and Rachel. Leah, the elder, we are told, had weak, bleary eyes which made her look very plain; but Rachel was beautiful, and Jacob fell in love with her. Laban had seemed very pleased to meet his nephew; but when Jacob asked his permission to marry Rachel, Laban insisted that first he must work without any pay for seven years. Jacob was ready to agree to any conditions; and he "served seven years for Rachel; and they seemed unto him but a few days, for the love he had to her."

At the end of the seven years Jacob went to his uncle to claim Rachel as his wife; but Laban, who found his nephew extremely useful, played an unkind trick on him. He told Jacob that it was not the custom for a younger daughter to marry before her elder sister, and so, if Jacob wanted to marry Rachel he must also marry Leah. And more than that, Laban refused to let Jacob marry at all unless he agreed to work for him for another seven years. There was nothing for it except to obey. Jacob therefore married both Laban's daughters and continued to work for him. Laban's mean trick, and the tricks which Jacob played on his brother, show that the people were still very backward. They had not learned—and some people even today have not learned—what the great leaders who came afterwards were to learn: the meaning of goodness and wisdom.

In the meantime, as the years went by, Leah had a number of sons. For a long time Rachel, the wife Jacob really loved, had no children. Then she gave birth to a son who was called Joseph; and much later—after the family had left Haran—she had one other son, Benjamin, the youngest of Jacob's family. And because Jacob loved Rachel so much more than he loved Leah, he loved Rachel's children better than Leah's. This made Leah and her sons jealous of Rachel and her sons; and so the story of family jealousy was repeated.

In the meantime, Jacob was longing to return to his own country. He had worked for his uncle so well that Laban had become rich in herds and flocks, and no longer needed Jacob's help. So Laban put no further obstacles in his nephew's way. He even gave him some of his beasts in payment for all he had done.

And so Jacob, with Leah, Rachel and their children, set out for home; but, as they journeyed, Jacob began to fear the meeting which must take place between himself and his brother. He had no idea if Esau would try to kill him and injure the women and children; but he thought that possibly a present might help Esau to forget his anger. Jacob therefore sent a party of his servants on ahead with some of his finest camels, asses, sheep and goats. Then he divided the rest of his company into two separate camps; for he hoped that if the worst happened and Esau led an army against him, the people in one of the camps would escape.

Esau made no attempt to attack either of the camps; and Jacob felt safe to go on. He took the women and children across a ford which divided them from his home country; and then he spent one night entirely alone. During that night he had another strange dream. He dreamed that an immensely strong man, who looked like an angel, came up to him and started to wrestle with him. The two of them struggled all night long; and towards morning Jacob was injured, but he refused to give way. Then his opponent said to him: "Let me go, for the day breaketh." But Jacob said, "I will not let thee go, except thou bless me." The stranger said, "What is thy name?" and Jacob told him. Then the stranger said, "Thy name shall be called no more Jacob, but Israel: for as a prince hast thou power with God and with men, and hast prevailed."

The meaning of Jacob's dream is not very clear. It could mean, of course, that because he still felt guilty at having cheated Esau out of his birthright and his blessing, he also felt that he must earn a blessing of his own. Then, too, it could mean that he had fought with a power stronger than himself and had won; that is to say, he had won a victory against his past wrongdoing.

The name "Israel" may mean "he who strives with God". But it may also mean "God strives", or "the champion of God"; and so the descendants of Jacob were known by his new name— Israelites.

Next day, we are told, Jacob recrossed the ford and went to face his brother; and when they met Esau showed at once that he bore his brother no ill-will. As soon as he saw Jacob approaching, he "ran to meet him, and embraced him, and fell on his neck, and kissed him: and they wept." He would not even take the gift which Jacob had sent him, saying, "I have enough, my brother; keep that thou hast unto thyself."

And yet, although Esau had generously forgiven Jacob, the trouble caused by jealousy in Jacob's family had only just begun. Foolishly, Jacob showed that he loved Rachel's children more than Leah's; and he made his preference clear by giving his favourite son, Joseph, a specially fine wide-sleeved coat—or robe —made of cloth of different colours. A robe of this kind was often worn by the man who would one day become leader of his tribe, and was taken as a sign that the wearer did not have to work.

The gift made Joseph, who was still only a boy, rather too pleased with himself. In fact, he had a dream one night which showed that he had begun to feel better than his elder brothers. In the morning he described his dream to them: "Behold, we were binding sheaves in the field, and, lo, my sheaf arose, and also stood upright; and, behold, your sheaves stood round about, and made obeisance to my sheaf." The people of those days believed that dreams foretold the future; and this dream could only mean that one day Joseph would rule over his brothers. A few nights later Joseph had another dream of the same kind. In this second dream, the sun and the moon—his father and mother —and eleven stars—his brothers—all bowed down to him.

Even Jacob was a little shocked to think that in the future he might have to bow down to his own son; but Joseph's elder brothers were so furious that they decided to do away with him. They plotted together to kill Joseph and afterwards to tell Jacob that the boy had been killed and eaten by a wild beast. This they would have done had not one of them been more merciful than the rest. The merciful brother persuaded the others not to kill Joseph but to sell him as a slave to some foreign traders. Then they killed an animal and spattered its blood on Joseph's robe, which they had taken from him before he was sold. When they showed the blood-stained robe to their father, Jacob believed that his favourite son was dead, and he refused to be comforted.

The Bible gives two versions of this story. In one, the merciful brother is Judah, although he is cruel enough to sell Joseph into slavery and to allow his father to mourn him as dead. In the second version Reuben is the kindly brother. He persuades the others to leave Joseph in a deep pit in the ground, meaning to return later in secret and rescue him. But Reuben arrives too late. Slave traders have discovered the boy and taken him away; and Reuben, who mourns for Joseph, is too frightened to explain to Jacob what has really happened.

According to the Bible, Joseph was taken to Egypt; and there he was sold as a slave to Potiphar, one of the most important men in the country. Potiphar was captain of the guard to the pharaoh, as the king of Egypt was called. He was so pleased with his new slave's ability that when Joseph grew older he gave him a position of trust in his household. Under Joseph's direction everything went well; and Potiphar promoted Joseph to be the overseer not only of his household but of all his estates.

By this time Joseph had become a very handsome man; and Potiphar's wife, who had grown rather bored with her husband, found him most attractive. Joseph would have nothing to do with her, and he told her so. As Potiphar's wife was a very vain and proud woman Joseph's neglect annoyed her so much that she determined to punish him. She therefore made false charges against him to her husband, and complained to him that Joseph— his Hebrew servant—had insulted her. Potiphar, who believed what his wife told him, had the Hebrew flung into prison.

Joseph remained in prison for many years; and he might have stayed there for the rest of his life if his ability to understand dreams had not come to his rescue. It so happened that two of the pharaoh's servants, his chief butler and his chief baker, had also been put in prison. Each of these men had a curious dream, and each asked Joseph if he could explain what it meant. Joseph told the baker that his dream meant that the pharaoh would have him executed. The butler, however, was to be more fortunate, for *his* dream meant that the pharaoh would soon order his release and give him back his post. And Joseph asked the butler, when he was restored to favour, to beg the pharaoh for his release. "For indeed I was stolen away out of the land of the Hebrews", he said; "and here also have I done nothing that they should put me into the dungeon."

Joseph's explanation of the two dreams proved to be correct. The unfortunate baker was taken away and hanged, and the butler was released and taken back into favour. The butler was so delighted to have his old post once more that he forgot that he had intended to ask for Joseph's release. Another two years went by; and then the pharaoh himself began to have strange dreams.

Nobody could interpret—or explain—these dreams, which worried the pharaoh exceedingly, until the butler remembered Joseph, who was still in prison.

When the butler told his master that Joseph had been able to interpret his dream and the baker's the pharaoh immediately sent for Joseph, and described two dreams to him. In the first dream, he said, he had seen seven sleek, fat cows come out of the Nile, and after them came seven lean, starved-looking cows. The lean cows ate the sleek cows; but after their meal the lean cows looked just as starved as they had before. The second dream was something like the first. In it, the pharaoh had seen seven full ears of wheat growing on a single stalk; and then he had seen seven withered ears, which had devoured the full ears.

"And Joseph said unto Pharaoh, The dream of Pharaoh is one: God hath shewed Pharaoh what he is about to do." The seven sleek cows and the seven full ears of wheat meant, said Joseph, that for the next seven years the Egyptian cattle and crops would flourish and the people would be well fed. The seven lean cows and the seven withered ears of wheat meant that the years of plenty would be followed by seven years of famine. "And for that the dream was doubled unto Pharaoh twice; it is because the thing is established by God, and God will shortly bring it to pass." Joseph did more than interpret the pharaoh's dreams; he also advised him how to deal with the situation. The best thing to do, he told the pharaoh, would be to appoint somebody "discreet and wise", somebody who would see to it that storehouses were filled with grain and other food during the years of plenty so that the people could eat during the years of famine.

"And the thing," the Bible story adds, "was good in the eyes of Pharaoh, and in the eyes of all his servants. And Pharaoh said unto his servants, Can we find such a one as this is, a man in whom the Spirit of God is? And Pharaoh said unto Joseph, For as much as God hath shewed thee all this, there is none so discreet and wise as thou art: Thou shalt be over my house, and according unto thy word shall all my people be ruled: only in the throne will I be greater than thou. And Pharaoh said unto Joseph, See, I have set thee over all the land of Egypt. And Pharaoh took off his ring from his hand, and put it upon Joseph's hand, and arrayed him in vestures of fine linen, and put a gold chain about his neck. And he made him to ride in the second chariot which he had; and they cried before him, Bow the knee: and he made him ruler over all the land of Egypt."

So Joseph, once a Hebrew slave, became the pharaoh's viceroy —or second-in-command. The ceremony described in the Bible is what actually took place when a pharaoh promoted one of his servants to be his viceroy. In recent years ancient wall paintings have been discovered in Egypt in one of which this very ceremony is shown. In the painting the pharaoh can be seen seated on his throne, while two servants stand below him dressing the viceroy in a fine linen robe and placing a gold chain of office round his neck.

At the period Joseph is thought to have lived, which is some time after 1700 B.C.,* Egypt was ruled by invading tribes from Syria and Palestine. The invaders were the Hyksos ("Hyksos" means "chiefs of foreign lands") who belonged to the same Semitic race as the Hebrew shepherd people. The Hyksos armies had overrun the country and enslaved the Egyptian people; and they had set a pharaoh of their own race on the throne. The pharaoh in the Bible story would have been a Hyksos king and not an Egyptian, although the Bible refers to him and all his subjects as Egyptians.

The Hyksos, who were in power for nearly two hundred years, introduced into Egypt the war-horse and the swift horse-drawn chariot. They were always afraid that one day the enslaved Egyptians would rise against them and drive them out of the country; and so they turned the land to the east of the delta of the Nile into a vast armed camp.

A man as important as Joseph had become would have to marry a woman of high rank; and the Bible tells us that the

* Or B.C.E. (Before the Common Era), the form used by some Jews.

pharaoh gave Joseph in marriage Asenath, the daughter of a priest, and that they had two sons. Although in the Bible the pharaoh speaks of "God", this means one of the gods whom he and his priests worshipped; but Joseph worshipped the one God, as had Abraham, Isaac and Jacob before him.

The Bible also tells us that Joseph's interpretation of the pharaoh's dreams was absolutely right. Yet, although dreams play such an important part in Joseph's story, elsewhere in the Bible we hear very little about them. This is probably because in very early days the Hebrews, like other people, believed that dreams were specially sent to warn them of the future. Later on, however, when their ideas were less primitive, the Hebrew leaders taught them that it was far better to try to lead good lives than to pay attention to dreams.

In the meantime, Joseph had done exactly what he set out to do. During the seven years of plenty his servants saved and stored an immense amount of grain, so that when the years of famine came —as they did—there was plenty of food for everybody.

The famine spread far beyond the borders of Egypt, and people in other lands who heard that there was food in Egypt flocked to buy it. Among the men who journeyed to Egypt in search of food were Joseph's ten elder brothers, "for the famine was in the land of Canaan".

We can picture quite clearly the appearance of these travellers. About seventy years ago a wall painting was discovered in an ancient Egyptian tomb which shows a wandering shepherd chief and his tribe being presented to an Egyptian nobleman by his servants. An inscription on the painting, which dates from about 1900 B.C., explains that the strangers are "Sand-dwellers", or Semites (and the Hebrews were a Semitic people). They are lighter-skinned than the Egyptians and are differently dressed. The Egyptian servants wear white loin-cloths which resemble short skirts; but the strangers wear brightly striped clothes. Some of the men, who have thick dark hair and pointed beards, wear kilts, or tunics reaching to their knees, and sandals on their feet.

The women, whose long dark hair is held by a narrow white ribbon across the forehead, wear longer tunics and instead of sandals they have soft ankle-length boots. There are children in the party, too, wearing plain coloured tunics, and two of the smallest are carried on the back of an ass in a basket made of animal skins. The men are armed with bows and arrows and spears; but one of them also carries a musical instrument, a lyre—which is something like a small harp—with eight strings.

Joseph's brothers would have looked much the same as the men in the wall painting. The Bible tells us that Joseph was present when they arrived and that he recognised them at once. They had not greatly changed, but Joseph was entirely different; and they did not recognise in the handsome, powerful viceroy of Egypt who stood before them, the boy they had treated so cruelly. When they bowed low before him, Joseph pretended not to know them. Instead, he spoke curtly to them, accusing them of being spies from a foreign country. This, the brothers denied. "Thy servants, are twelve brethren", said one of them, "the sons of one man in the land of Canaan; and, behold, the youngest is this day with our father, and one is not." Roughly, Joseph told them that he would put their story to the test. One among them should stay behind as a hostage, while the rest returned to Canaan to fetch the youngest brother, of whom they had spoken.

The brothers dared not refuse, although they knew that Jacob, who dearly loved his youngest son, Benjamin, would hate to part with him even for the shortest time. One of them—Simeon—remained in Egypt, while the others made ready for the journey, tying on the backs of their asses the sacks of grain which they had bought. They did not know that Joseph had ordered his steward to put in the mouth of each sack the money he had received for the food it contained.

On the way home the brothers found the money. The discovery terrified them, for they did not see how they could prove to the viceroy on their return that they were honest men and had not stolen the money. When they reached home and told their father that the viceroy had ordered them to take Benjamin back to Egypt Jacob at first refused. But when all the grain they had brought with them had been eaten and the tribe was faced again with famine, they persuaded him to agree, promising to guard Benjamin with their lives.

As they neared Egypt the brothers became more and more anxious. The first thing they did when they reached Joseph's house was to find his steward and tell him that somebody had put back the money in their sacks. The steward replied: "Peace be to you, fear not: your God and the God of your father, hath given you treasure in your sacks: I had your money." Then the steward brought their brother Simeon to them, and told them that they were all to eat with Joseph that day.

When Joseph arrived home at noon he greeted his brothers, though still as a stranger. "Is your father well, the old man of whom ye spake?" he asked. "Is he yet alive? And they answered, Thy servant our father is in good health, he is yet alive. And they bowed down their heads, and made obeisance. And he lifted up his eyes, and saw his brother Benjamin, his mother's son, and said, Is this your younger brother, of whom ye spake unto me? And he said, God be gracious unto thee, my son. And Joseph made haste; for his bowels did yearn upon his brother: and he sought where to weep; and he entered into his chamber, and wept there. And he washed his face, and went out, and refrained himself, and said, Set on bread." Joseph always sat by himself at table, for he was a Hebrew, and it was against the custom of the Egyptians to eat with a Hebrew. The brothers sat together at a separate table; and they were amazed to find that their places had been set in the exact order of their age, with the eldest at the head of the table. Food was brought to them from Joseph's table, and Benjamin was given the largest share.

When they had eaten Joseph told his steward to fill the brothers' sacks and to put back the money, as he had done before; and he was to place in the mouth of Benjamin's sack not only the money but also his own silver cup. And then, as soon as the brothers had started for home, Joseph ordered the steward to ride after them, search their sacks and, when he found the silver cup, to bring them all back in disgrace.

The frightened brothers tried in vain to prove to Joseph that they were innocent of theft. After much discussion he seemed to relent, and told them that they might all go free, all except the one in whose sack the cup had been found. The culprit, said Joseph, must stay in Egypt as a slave.

The brothers could not bear this, for they knew that if they returned home without Benjamin it would kill their father. And so Judah (who in one of the two Bible versions was the merciful brother) courageously tried to take Benjamin's place. "Now therefore, I pray thee, let thy servant abide instead of the lad a bondman to my lord; and let the lad go up with his brethren. For how shall I go up to my father, and the lad be not with me? lest peradventure I see the evil that shall come on my father. Then Joseph could not refrain himself before all of them that stood by him; and he cried, Cause every man to go out from me. And there stood no man with him, while Joseph made himself known unto his brethren. And he wept aloud: and the Egyptians and the house of Pharaoh heard. And Joseph said unto his brethren, I am Joseph; doth my father yet live? And his brethren could not answer him; for they were troubled at his presence. And Joseph said unto his brethren, Come near to me, I pray you. And they came near. And he said, I am Joseph your brother, whom ye sold into Egypt. Now therefore, be not grieved, nor angry with your-selves, that ye sold me hither: for God did send me before you to preserve life. For these two years hath the famine been in the land: and yet there are five years, in the which there shall neither be earing nor harvest. . . . Haste ye and go up to my father, and say unto him, Thus sayeth thy son Joseph, God hath made me lord of all Egypt: come down unto me, tarry not: And thou shalt dwell in the land of Goshen, and thou shalt be near unto me, thou, and thy children, and thy children's children, and thy flocks, and thy herds, and all that thou hast: And there will I nourish thee. . . .

And he fell upon his brother Benjamin's neck, and wept; and Benjamin wept upon his neck. Moreover he kissed all his brethren, and wept upon them: and after that his brethren talked with him."

When Jacob, who by now was an old man, learned the wonderful news, he said: "It is enough; Joseph my son is yet alive: I will go and see him before I die." And Jacob and the rest of his people journeyed into Egypt; and when he heard they were coming "Joseph made ready his chariot, and went up to meet Israel his father, to Goshen, and presented himself unto him; and he fell on his neck, and wept on his neck a good while. And Israel said unto Joseph, Now let me die, since I have seen thy face, and because thou art yet alive."

When the pharaoh was told that Joseph's family were shepherds who could care for his flocks he gave them permission to live in Goshen, a part of the country which was rich in pasture land. "And Joseph placed his father and his brethren, and gave them a possession in the land of Egypt, in the best of the land, as Pharaoh had commanded."

The story of Joseph with its happy ending sounds almost too good to be true. It may well have happened, of course; but it is possible that it was told as a parable to show both the harm which jealousy can cause and the beauty of true forgiveness. But whether the story happened exactly as it is written or not, we do know that during the rule of the Hyksos a tribe of Hebrew wanderers (Semites like themselves) arrived in Egypt, and this seems to suggest that the story of Joseph has some basis of fact. The Hyksos, fearful always of an Egyptian rising, welcomed the Hebrews and allowed them to settle in Goshen, a stretch of fertile land between the delta of the Nile and the Arabian Desert, hoping that in the event of a rebellion the Hebrews would come to their aid.

Eventually the Egyptians did revolt. After a series of battles they defeated the Hyksos tyrants and drove them out of the country. The Hebrews took no part in the fighting; and the

Egyptians allowed them to stay on in Goshen where they lived for many years.

In the meantime, Jacob had long since been dead. Before his death he had blessed each of his twelve sons—Reuben, Simeon, Levi, Judah, Zebulun, Issachar, Dan, Gad, Asher, Naphtali, Joseph and Benjamin. The Bible tells us that the Hebrews were divided into twelve tribes and that each tribe was named after one of Jacob's sons.

CHAPTER III

MOSES

Many hundreds of years went by before the Israelites were heard of again. They must have been peaceful years, and the Israelites grew very numerous. But then, we are told, "there arose a new king over Egypt, which knew not Joseph". The story of Joseph had been forgotten; and this new pharaoh—an Egyptian—was very suspicious of the foreigners who were still living in Goshen. It was true that the Israelites had not fought against the Egyptians, but they belonged to the same race as the hated Hyksos tyrants, and so the Egyptians feared them.

Fear often leads to acts of cruelty and oppression; and the pharaoh's fear that one day the Israelites might grow strong enough to oppose him led him to decide to make them slaves. The pharaoh was most probably Rameses II, whose long reign lasted for sixty-seven years, from about 1301 to 1234 B.C. Rameses, who was known as "the Great", was very fond of building monuments to celebrate his victories over his enemies. Among the monuments were many statues of himself, and he also built a number of strongly fortified cities. For all this work he needed labourers, and by enslaving the Israelites, he would force them to work all day making bricks, without giving them any pay. The Israelites, who were most of them shepherds, had never done this kind of work before, and they hated it. The Bible mentions two cities—Pithom and Raamses—which the slaves were forced to build, and says that they were treated most cruelly. They were given plenty of food in order to keep them well enough to work: but if they did not make the right number of bricks every day they were brutally beaten.

The bricks were made of clay, dug from the river bank, and straw; and an ancient wall painting discovered in a rock tomb near the Egyptian city of Thebes shows what the work was like. In the painting light-skinned labourers are seen, some of them carrying jars of water, others spreading mortar between bricks and building a wall, while a dark-skinned Egyptian overseer sits watching them, with a rod in his hand.

Although the Israelites were made to work so desperately hard they continued to multiply; and the pharaoh was more fearful than ever that one day they would join his enemies and revolt against him. And so, the Bible tells us, he decided to get rid of them. He issued a decree that in future every Hebrew boy child born alive should be killed at birth. Soon after the decree was made a son was born to one of the slaves and his wife, who was called Jochebed. The couple already had two children, a son named Aaron, and a daughter, Miriam. When the baby was born Jochebed kept his birth a secret from everybody except her husband and children, for fear that he would be put to death. Then, we are told, "she took for him an ark of bulrushes, and daubed it with slime and with pitch, and put the child therein; and she laid it in the flags by the river's brink."

The description of the basket—or cradle—in which Jochebed left her baby son is like another, much earlier, description which was given by a Semitic king called Sargon. An inscription discovered in recent years relates that Sargon's mother, who wanted to conceal his birth, put him "in a little box made of reeds, sealing its lid with pitch". She then placed the box in the river, where it was found by a water-carrier, who rescued and adopted the baby.

The story about Jochebed's baby son may have been copied from the earlier story; but the baby son was real enough. He was Moses, the greatest of all the Jewish heroes, the leader of the Israelites and their law-giver. According to the Bible story, the basket in which his mother placed him was discovered by an Egyptian princess, who drew the baby out of the water and decided to adopt him, since she had no children of her own; and the name "Moses" probably comes from an Egyptian word meaning "son" or "boy", although it may possibly come from a Hebrew word meaning "draw out". The Bible story goes on to say that the baby's sister, Miriam, who had seen the princess lift him out of his cradle, came forward and offered to find a nurse for him. The princess agreed and, instead of fetching an ordinary nurse, Miriam went in search of her mother. So Moses spent the first few years of his life among his own people, and his mother taught him all she could about them. Later on, Jochebed "brought him unto Pharaoh's daughter, and he became her son".

It was the custom in ancient Egypt for children of royal or noble birth to be brought up by nurses, who looked after them for several years, not in a royal palace, but in their own homes. And Moses, when he left his mother, was given the education and training of an Egyptian nobleman. He must have learned to read and write and must have studied mathematics and other subjects; but although the Egyptian priests would have taught him about the many gods and goddesses which the Egyptians worshipped, Moses never forgot that he was a Hebrew.

He also knew that the Hebrews were slaves. One day, "when Moses was grown", says the Bible, "he went out unto his brethren, and looked on their burdens; and he spied an Egyptian smiting an Hebrew, one of his brethren". The sight of the beaten slave made him so angry that he completely lost his temper. In a burst of rage, he killed the Egyptian overseer and buried his body in the sand.

Moses knew that the pharaoh would think that the Egyptian

had only been doing his duty. When, therefore, he killed the overseer, Moses had been defying the pharaoh who had set the man over the slaves; and for such a crime he would probably be punished. For this reason, or because he felt guilty—as indeed he did—Moses fled to Midian in the Arabian Desert. He was resting in a quiet spot after his hurried journey when seven young women, the daughters of a priest, came to draw water from a nearby well. A group of shepherds arrived at the same time, and they were trying to prevent the girls from drawing water when Moses sprang up and drove the shepherds away. The grateful girls took Moses to their father, whose name was Jethro; and in due course Moses married Zipporah, one of Jethro's daughters.

Moses then became a wandering shepherd and looked after his father-in-law's flocks. There is a legend which describes his special care for these animals. He always led the youngest animals out to pasture first, so that they could feed on the most juicy and tender grass. Next he led out beasts which were rather older and let them graze on the herbs which he knew were best for them. Finally he led out the strongest, fully-grown animals and gave them grass which was too tough for the others but which they could easily digest. And God, who had seen how well Moses cared for the flocks, knew that he would also be a good leader of men. "Then spake God", says the legend, "He that under-standeth how to pasture sheep, providing for each what is good for it, he shall pasture My people."

While Moses was tending his father-in-law's sheep, wandering from place to place in search of good pasture land, he had plenty of time to think; and his thoughts turned more and more to the idea of the one God. The Bible tells us that one day he saw a desert thorn bush which seemed to be on fire and yet was never burnt up. Moses went closer to examine this strange sight. As he did so a strong feeling came over him that he was treading on holy ground and that, as a sign of reverence, he should take off his sandals and walk barefoot. And then, from out of the thorn bush he seemed to hear the voice of God, saying: "I am the God of thy father, the God of Abraham, the God of Isaac, and the God of Jacob. And Moses hid his face; for he was afraid to look upon God. And the Lord said, I have surely seen the affliction of my people which are in Egypt, and have heard their cry by reason of their taskmasters; for I know their sorrows; And I am come down to deliver them out of the hand of the Egyptians, and to bring them up out of that land unto a good land and a large, unto a land flowing with milk and honey; . . . Come, now therefore, and I will send thee unto Pharaoh, that thou mayest bring forth thy people the children of Israel out of Egypt."

Moses shrank back from such a task. "Who am I, that I should go unto Pharaoh, and that I should bring forth the children of Israel out of Egypt?" he asked. He was slow and halting of speech, he said, and he could not argue with the pharaoh or force him to release his slaves. But God promised Moses that he would be given the strength to carry out his mission and that he would have the help of his brother, Aaron; and Moses had the faith to believe that he could, indeed, do all that was required of him.

There are many people who are sure that Moses really did hear the voice of God speaking to him from the midst of the burning bush. Throughout history there have been deeply religious men and women who seem to have heard inner voices warning and guiding them, almost driving them into doing things which, if left to themselves, they would not have dared to attempt. Moses himself was driven to undertake a task so difficult and so dangerous that the very idea of it terrified him, and yet he agreed to do it.

There are other people who think that it was not God's voice but the voice of his own conscience that he heard, urging him to do what he knew in his heart he ought to do. There are people, too, who think that he was mistaken in imagining that the thorn bush was actually on fire. In desert country, as they know, a kind of mistletoe with brilliant red blossoms is often found growing on certain prickly bushes, and when the mistletoe is in bloom the whole bush is covered in flaming colour. If Moses saw the red mistletoe in full bloom he may well have mistaken it for fire; and the strong feeling that he was treading on holy ground may have prevented him from examining the bush more closely.

But whichever way we look at it, one thing is absolutely clear. Moses, despite his fears, realised that unless he became a leader his people might remain slaves in Egypt for ever. As a young man he had fled from the pharaoh's anger; but he was older now, and he knew that his people needed him.

And so, with faith in God and high courage, he went back to Egypt to plead their cause. With his brother Aaron he went fearlessly into the pharaoh's presence, crying: "Thus saith the Lord God of Israel. Let my people go."

The pharaoh, who had never heard of the God of Israel, scornfully refused. According to the Bible, he showed his power over his slaves by making them work harder than ever. Before, the slaves had been given the straw which they needed to make bricks; now, they had to find the straw themselves and yet make the same number of bricks each day. When they failed, as they frequently did, they were brutally punished.

When the slaves realised that their life was being made harder just because Moses was trying to get them released they began to wonder if they would not be better off as they were. Moses therefore found that he had two tasks instead of one. He had to persuade the pharaoh to let his slaves go, and also to persuade the slaves that they ought to go. He fulfilled the first task, the Bible tells us, by warning the pharaoh that until he gave his consent God would send one plague after another to afflict the Egyptian people. There was a plague of flies which darkened the air and settled on man and beast. There was a plague of frogs which covered the earth; a plague of locusts which devoured the crops; a cattle disease which killed many of the finest beasts. And, more alarming than these, the waters of the Nile changed suddenly from clear water into blood.

Troubles of this kind were not uncommon in the Middle East, and at certain times of the year the flood waters of the Nile turned a dark reddish-brown. The people thought that their troubles were caused by the gods; but this year things seemed far worse than ever before, for Moses was at hand with his warning that God would punish Egypt until the pharaoh let His people go. The pharaoh began to waver; first he appeared to relent, but he quickly changed his mind. Then came the worst of all the plagues. For three days a sandstorm raged, so thick that people could scarcely breathe. During the darkness of the storm a sickness broke out, especially among the children, many of whom died within a few hours. When his own child—his eldest son—caught the disease and died the pharaoh gave up the fight. He sent for Moses and Aaron, saying to them: "Rise up, and get you forth from among my people, both ye and the children of Israel; and go, serve the Lord, as ye have said."

Moses had no time to lose, for he knew very well that the pharaoh would probably change his mind yet again. Hurriedly he went among the slaves, entreating them to follow him without delay. He had spoken to them many times before, and his influence over them had become strong enough for them to obey without question. After eating a hasty meal of meat and herbs they were ready. The women had been preparing bread, which had not yet been baked; and so each man added to the bundle which he carried on his back a portion of the dough.

The Exodus, as the departure from Egypt is called, is celebrated every year by Jews all over the world in the festival of the Passover. The festival, which lasts for a week, is called Passover because God is said to have punished the Egyptians but to have "passed over"—or saved—the Hebrew slaves. During the festival it is the custom for Jews to eat special, flat crisp biscuits instead of bread in memory of the dough which the slaves carried with them and which was baked into flat biscuits by the heat of the sun.

The Exodus, we think, took place about the year 1290 B.C. Moses led his people towards Canaan, the country where Abraham had settled and his family had lived until famine drove them into Egypt. The quickest route to Canaan would have been by

way of Gaza on the coast of the Mediterranean Sea; but the
country in between was in the hands of the warlike Philistine
people, who could easily have beaten the fugitives in battle.
Moses therefore chose a much longer route, which took them
very far to the south and through the desert.

The first stage of their journey brought them to a point at
which they had to cross water. This point may have been a
marshy lake which no longer exists called the "Reed" Sea; or it
may have been the Red Sea, which washes the eastern coast of
Egypt and at its northern end is split into two gulfs by the
Peninsula of Sinai. Moses probably decided to camp on the shores
of one of these gulfs—the Gulf of Suez; but there was no time to
rest. In the distance the thunder of Egyptian war-chariots could
be heard; for now that the plagues had lifted the pharaoh had
decided to send an army after his slaves to bring them back.

The Israelites were terrified. If they dashed into the sea they
would surely all be drowned; and if they stayed they would be
captured. But Moses, who was not afraid, cried out to them in
a strong voice: "Fear ye not, stand still, and see the salvation of
the Lord, which he will shew to you today." And then, as
though in answer to a prayer, a sudden east wind arose and swept
the water aside, so that the Israelites crossed over to the Peninsula
on dry land.

It is not uncommon for water to be blown aside by a powerful
wind, leaving a passage which is clear or shallow enough for
people to wade across. But to the Israelites, who believed that
natural happenings were the work of God, this was a miracle. And
scarcely had they reached the other side when the wind dropped.
They paused for a moment in their flight to see if the Egyptians
were following. They were; but as soon as the wind dropped the
water came flooding back, and the Egyptian chariots were
swamped, and every man and every horse was drowned.

The Bible tells us that, led by Miriam, the sister of Moses and
Aaron, the Israelites sang a song of thankfulness and praise to God
who had delivered them: "I will sing unto the Lord, for he hath

triumphed gloriously: the horse and his rider hath he thrown into the sea. The Lord is my strength and song, and he is become my salvation: he is my God, and I will prepare him an habitation; my father's God, and I will exalt him. The Lord is a man of war: the Lord is his name."

The song goes on in the same warlike manner, praising God for taking revenge on the wicked Egyptians. The peoples of these days saw nothing wrong in taking revenge. Nobody would have been shocked, for example, if Joseph, instead of forgiving his brothers, had killed them for their former cruelty towards him. But the Jewish rabbis of a later age taught that forgiveness is right and revenge is wrong. One of their legends tells how, while the Egyptians drowned, the angels began to sing praises to God. But God stopped them, saying: "The Egyptians are also my children and they are drowning; this is no time for songs of oy."

When the Israelites had rested after their safe crossing Moses led them southwards keeping near to the sea-shore and making for Mount Horeb (or Mount Sinai as it is also called), not far from the spot at which he had had his vision of the burning bush. He had obeyed his inward voice and had brought the Israelites out of Egypt; but he had a far longer task ahead. The Israelites had been slaves for so long that they had lost the will to think and act for themselves; and whenever things went wrong they gave way to panic and cried out to Moses that they had been better off in Egypt. They were often short of food and drink in the desert, and they grumbled because they had to march each day until they came to an oasis or a water-hole where they could camp for the night. Moses realised that there was no hope of a good future for these people unless he could help them to become independent. He had to turn a pack of frightened, discontented slaves into a free and confident nation; and in the meantime he had to keep them from starving to death in the desert.

Scholars of our own age have been able to trace from the description given in the Bible a large part of the Israelites' route.

The names of some of the oases at which they camped have been changed, but the fertile spots themselves still exist. At one of their stopping-places (it is called in the Bible "Elim") they found welcome shade from the palm trees which sheltered twelve wells. But although there was plenty of water there was nothing to eat, and the people thought longingly of the food they had been given in Egypt. "Then," according to the Bible, "said the Lord unto Moses, Behold, I will rain bread from heaven for you. . . . At even* ye shall eat flesh, and in the morning ye shall be filled with bread; and ye shall know that I am the Lord your God."

What happened next seemed another miracle to the starving Israelites, but there is also a natural explanation for it. The Exodus took place during the spring, a time when many birds fly from Africa to Europe for the warm summer months. They fly across the Red Sea and alight on the shores to rest before continuing their flight. This migration—or flight—of the birds goes on for some time; and evening after evening the Israelites found small birds on the shore which were so weary that they could easily be caught and killed. "And it came to pass," says the Bible, "that at even the quails came up, and covered the camp; and in the morning the dew lay round about the host. And when the dew that lay was gone up, behold, upon the face of the wilderness there lay a small round thing, as small as the hoar frost on the ground." The Israelites could not imagine what this thing was. "And Moses said unto them, This is the bread which the Lord hath given you to eat." So the Israelites gathered and ate this strange bread. It tasted of honey, and they called it "manna". Every morning afterwards the ground about their camp was covered with manna, and each morning the Israelites gathered a fresh supply.

In the Sinai Peninsula manna is still to be found today. It is a kind of sap which drips from the tamarisk tree when the bark of the tree is pierced by certain small insects. The sap falls to the

* Evening.

ground and does indeed look rather like frost; and wandering desert tribes gather and eat it as did the Israelites of old.

The discovery of manna was a fresh sign to the Israelites that God was with them. For a time they ceased their complaints and, led by Moses, they worshipped God. When their leader was with them their faith was strong; but there were times when he climbed Mount Sinai—the "Holy Mount" as it is called in the Bible—to pray and to meditate; and when Moses was not with them the people began to imitate the customs of their pagan neighbours.

On Mount Sinai Moses had his grandest vision; for at the summit of the Holy Mount, says the Bible, "Moses spake, and God answered him by a voice." When he came down from the mountain, we are told, he carried with him two tablets of stone on which were engraved the Ten Commandments, the rules which are held in the greatest respect today by Christians as well as Jews. The Commandments open with the well-known words: "I am the Lord thy God, which have brought thee out of the land of Egypt, out of the house of bondage." They proclaim that God is God alone, and that His people must never worship idols, as the pagans did. The Fourth Commandment gave the Israelites a new idea, the idea that everybody should have a weekly day of rest. "Remember the sabbath day, to keep it holy. Six days shalt thou labour, and do all thy work; but the seventh day is the sabbath of the Lord thy God." No one should work on the sabbath. It should be a day of rest for masters and servants alike, and even for the cattle. The rest of the Commandments are all concerned with everyday life. The people should look up to their parents, for example, and care for them when they were old. They should not kill. They should not steal, or try by any other means to get hold of something which belonged to somebody else. They should not bear "false witness"—tell an untruth—against anyone.

The Bible goes on to tell us that when Moses descended from the Holy Mount carrying the stone tablets he found to his disgust

Megiddo: (*above*) the stables excavated (*below*) reconstruction drawing of a large building (*both courtesy Oriental Institute, University of Chicago*)

The Moabite Stone (*courtesy the Louvre*)

that the Israelites had made an idol of gold in the shape of a calf and were worshipping it. In his anger he flung the tablets to the ground to show that the Israelites were not worthy of the laws he was bringing them, and the tablets were broken into fragments. Then he smashed the golden idol into tiny pieces.

For a long time Moses feared that God in His anger would destroy the people; but after they had sincerely repented of their idol worship, we are told that he begged God to forgive them, and that as a sign of His forgiveness God gave Moses the Commandments again.

The stone tablets on which the Commandments were engraved were then placed in a simple wooden chest or box called the Ark. The Ark itself was kept behind drawn curtains in the tabernacle, a building which looked rather like a tent. And Moses taught the people to reverence and obey the Commandments, which formed the most important part of their Law.

There are two versions of the Ten Commandments in the Bible. The first is in the Book of Exodus, which also describes the escape of the Israelites from Egypt, tells of their life in the desert, and gives a list of other laws. The second version is in the Book of Deuteronomy, which adds many more laws to the list. There are still more laws in the Book of Leviticus; and among these is one of the finest of them all. This law, which influences Jews and Christians alike, lays it down that no one shall take revenge or bear any grudge against anybody else, and ends with the famous words: "Thou shalt love thy neighbour as thyself."

From the arrangement in the Bible it looks as though all these laws were given to Moses by God; but a great many of them probably belong to later dates and were made by the leaders who came after Moses. We can see from the laws that the Israelites were taught that the worship of idols, and other pagan customs, were wicked and wrong. They were told, among other things, to lighten the burden of slavery. They were told to let the remembrance of their sufferings as strangers in Egypt make them kind and considerate towards all strangers. And they were told that they should devote themselves to serving God and obeying His laws and commandments: "Ye shall be unto me a kingdom of priests, and an holy nation."

The ideas which laws such as these contained were high and splendid; but time and time again the Israelites failed to live up to them. The men and women who followed Moses out of Egypt were weak and discontented; and Moses had to teach them to live and work together as a nation. He began to train them to rule themselves by giving a certain amount of responsibility to those men who could be trusted to use it wisely. He "chose able men out of all Israel, and made them heads over the people, rulers of thousands, rulers of hundreds, rulers of fifties, and rulers of tens. And they judged the people at all seasons: the hard causes they brought unto Moses, but every small matter they judged themselves."

One version of this story tells us that Moses had been advised by his father-in-law, Jethro, not to take upon himself the whole burden of governing the people; for Jethro, who had once been a pagan priest, had given up the worship of idols and now followed Moses in the worship of God. In another version Moses pleads with God to give him help. "And the Lord said unto Moses, Gather unto me seventy men of the elders of Israel, whom thou knowest to be the elders of the people, and officers over them; and bring them unto the tabernacle of the congregation, that they may stand there with thee. And I will come down and talk with thee there: and I will take of the spirit which is upon thee, and will put it upon them; and they shall bear the burden of the people with thee, that thou bear it not thyself alone."

Moses did as he was ordered; and the elders—the wise men he had chosen—received the spirit of God and began to prophesy—or preach—to the people. Two of the elders who had been chosen had not joined the rest. Their names were Eldad and Medad; but, although they had remained behind, they, too, felt the spirit, and they began to prophesy in the camp. Then a young man ran to the tent of meeting and told this to Joshua, one of the chosen, who was Moses' right-hand man. And Joshua complained to Moses that Eldad and Medad had no right to preach or to take any part in the government of the people. "My lord Moses, forbid them", said Joshua. "And Moses said unto him, Enviest thou for my sake? would God that all the Lord's people were prophets, and that the Lord would put his spirit upon them!" Moses' reply shows what a really great leader he was; for only the greatest would have been so willing to give up his powers to other men.

According to the Bible, Moses spent forty years teaching and training his people. During those years the older men and women among them had died; but their children had learned how to live as a free and independent nation. Only then were they ready to leave their wandering desert life and enter Canaan, the promised land. Other tribes were already living in Canaan. They were pagans who worshipped idols and still offered human sacrifices to their gods. The Israelites believed that God intended to punish the Canaanites for their evil ways by taking their land from them. They also thought that if they invaded Canaan they would be doing God's will.

Before they left the desert Moses sent a few men ahead to spy out the land, among them his trusted helper Joshua, who was to take his place as leader. Joshua returned with stories of a rich and fertile land; and, to prove it, his men were carrying baskets filled with fresh fruit which would not grow in the dry desert soil.

By this time Moses was a very old man. He knew that he himself would not enter Canaan; but, old and tired as he was, he had the strength to climb a mountain, Mount Nebo (or Mount Pisgah as it is also called), and from its height to look down on the promised land in all its richness. There on the mountain top he died; and the Bible tells us that "no man knoweth of his sepulchre unto this day".

There was no need for the Israelites to know where their leader's body lay buried. Neither they nor their descendants would ever forget him; and to this day he is remembered by Jews all over the world as Moses, the law-giver, the greatest of all their heroes. One of the old legends tells us that even God Himself praised Moses, in these words: "Thou hast said of Me, 'The Lord He is God: there is none else', and therefore shall I say of thee, 'And there arose not a prophet in Israel like unto Moses.' "

CHAPTER IV

THE JUDGES AND ISRAEL'S FIRST KING

THE BIBLE DOES not tell us very much about Joshua, the man who was chosen to lead the Israelites across the Jordan and into the promised land of Canaan (or Palestine). We know that he was brave and extremely loyal to Moses, his leader; but Moses was a hero—the greatest hero in Jewish Biblical history—and Joshua cannot be compared with him in greatness.

The country which the Israelites invaded under Joshua was only about one-sixth the size of England (or, to compare it with an American state, midway in size between New Jersey and Connecticut). It was a land of contrasts, with a central mountain-range running from north to south, cool in the heights and stiflingly hot in the valleys. During the spring, autumn and summer months there was plenty of rain, and in summer there was heavy dew; and to the Israelites, who were used to the sandy wastes of the desert, the country must have looked wonderfully fertile. The Canaanites—the various tribes who lived in the country—must have seemed very civilised. The Israelites had led a hard, rough life for many years; and everything they made—like their black tents woven from goats' hair—was made

c

for use. But the Canaanites were skilled in the working of bronze and other precious metals; they made beautifully decorated pottery; they built cities and surrounded them with thick, high walls; they drilled tunnels for water; and their scribes wrote letters on clay tablets. But the Israelites—at any rate at the start— had one big advantage over the Canaanites. They were united under their leader; but the Canaanites were divided into a number of small city-states, each state ruled by its own king, and none willing to join forces with the others.

When the Israelites crossed the Jordan into Canaan they carried with them their most treasured possession, the Ark which contained the tablets of the Law. They believed that God intended them to capture the country; but they found their way blocked by Jericho,* a fortified, walled city. According to the Bible story, Joshua obeyed an order from God as to how the city was to be taken. Every day for six days his men of war marched once round the city walls. In their midst was the Ark, which was guarded by seven priests who blew trumpets made of rams' horns. Instead of coming out to attack the Israelites, the people of Jericho remained invisible behind the shelter of the walls. They did not understand what was happening, and they were probably too frightened to move. On the seventh day Joshua's men circled the city seven times. Then the priests gave a signal—a long, loud blast on their trumpets; the Israelites raised their voices in a mighty shout; and at the sound, the walls of Jericho collapsed. The Israelites then rushed in and captured the city without any trouble.

In modern times archaeologists have made many important discoveries about Jericho. In the first few years of the twentieth century a German expedition found traces of two ancient walls, one within the other. The inner wall was about twelve feet thick and twenty feet high; the outer wall was not so thick but rather higher. But the members of the expedition could not tell when the walls were built or when they were destroyed. Some years

* Many places mentioned in this and subsequent chapters are shown on the map, p. 97.

later—in 1930—a British expedition led by Professor John Garstang tried to solve this problem. The task was more difficult than it might have been because the Germans, who did not know what others learned after them, had dug carelessly into the site and had left their finds in confusion. As Professor Garstang and his team realised, it was most important to dig with the greatest care; for the remains of one age are left on top of the remains of the age that went before it. And so it is often possible to discover the date at which one set of people lived from their pottery, jewellery and other objects.

From his study of the remains of the walls and of the pottery, bronze weapons and jewellery which he found, Professor Garstang decided that Jericho had probably been destroyed somewhere between 1400 and 1375 B.C. Other archaeologists suggested quite different dates; but nobody really knew the answer. It remained a puzzle until 1953, when Dr. Kathleen Kenyon, who was Director of the British School of Archaeology in Jerusalem and a lecturer at the University of London, directed some fresh excavations. After five years of careful work she came to the conclusion that Jericho was far older than Professor Garstang or the other archaeologists had thought; that it was in fact the earliest town yet discovered and excavated. Jericho's original walls had been built somewhere about 7,000 B.C., centuries before the Israelite invasion; and, since the city lay within an earthquake zone, its walls had probably been destroyed in earthquakes and rebuilt or repaired a number of times.

It is most likely, then, that the Israelites entered Canaan at the time of an earthquake which tumbled down the walls of Jericho for them. This seems even more probable when we read the Bible description of the crossing of the Jordan: "As they that bare the Ark were come unto Jordan . . . the waters which came down from above stood and rose up upon an heap very far . . . and the people passed over right against Jericho. And the priests that bare the ark of the covenant of the Lord stood firm on dry ground in the midst of Jordan, and all the Israelites passed over on dry ground, until all the people were passed clean over Jordan."

The disturbances caused by an earthquake would account for the drying up of the river, just as they would for the destruction of the walls. But the important thing to remember about the crossing of the Jordan and, earlier, of the Red Sea is that the Israelites were there at the right time.

The date of the Israelite invasion of Canaan was probably between 1250 and 1225 B.C. With the capture of Jericho the first obstacle had been overcome; but, although the interior of the country now lay open to the Israelites, they had many battles to fight. They chose to invade the high, mountainous country and, after bitter fighting, they succeeded in conquering it. The country was then divided into separate states, each state called after one of the tribes of Israel. The Bible sometimes mentions the states by the names of the tribes which occupied them; but it refers to them all together as "Israel".

The people of Israel settled down to farm their new land. They were masters of the mountainous country, but the Canaanites still held a number of strongly guarded cities in the plains. From time to time the Canaanites sallied forth in their powerful iron-plated chariots and attacked the Israelite settlements; and often the Israelites were defeated in battle. The trouble by this time was that the Israelites were no longer a united people. Each tribe was only interested in itself; and the tribes did not join forces and fight as one army.

Sometimes an Israelite hero appeared, who led the men of his own tribe to victory against the enemy; but these heroes were not national leaders, as Moses and Joshua had been.

The heroes are called Judges in the Bible. They were not judges as we know them today, but chieftains or leaders. There was one woman among the judges. Her name was Deborah, and she lived in the hill country of the tribe of Ephraim. Deborah, who was wise and courageous, was a deeply religious woman. Her faith was so strong that when people came to her for guidance, as they often did, they seemed to hear the word of God in her voice. Because of her loving care of them Deborah was known as a "mother" in Israel. During her lifetime the people were being oppressed by a Canaanite ruler called Jabin and by Sisera, the general of Jabin's army. Deborah encouraged the people to revolt; not only the people of her own tribe but of other tribes as well; and she summoned a general—Barak—and ordered him in the name of God to lead the troops into battle. And Barak, who knew what the people felt about Deborah, refused to go without her. "If thou wilt go with me, then I will go," he said to her; "but if thou wilt not go with me, then I will not go. And she said, I will surely go with thee . . ."

When Sisera learned that Barak was arming against him he called out nine hundred of his famous iron chariots and a powerful army of men. "And Deborah said unto Barak, Up; for this is the day in which the Lord hath delivered Sisera into thine hand: is not the Lord gone out before thee?" Inspired by Deborah's presence Barak attacked Sisera's forces on the broad plain of Jezreel, which lies between Samaria and the mountains of Galilee, and he won a sweeping victory over the oppressors.

Another famous Israelite leader was Gideon, of the tribe of Manasseh. Gideon, like Deborah, was very religious and cared deeply for the welfare of the people. He was also a brilliant general; but his faith convinced him that God alone would give the Israelites victory over their enemies. He had summoned his people to fight the army of the Midianites which was encamped in the Valley of Jezreel, and 32,000 men from his own tribe of Manasseh and from three northern tribes—Asher, Zebulon and Naphtali—had answered his call. But Gideon wanted to prove that power belonged to God and not to man, and that with God's help the smallest army could prevail against the largest. He therefore cut down his own army from 32,000 to three hundred. With this tiny force he routed the Midianites, who fled in panic towards the Jordan Valley.

Gideon had been called "the deliverer"; but he himself looked on God as the only deliverer. There is a story in the Bible that after his great victory he was invited to become king over all the Israelite tribes; but he refused, saying that God alone was Israel's king.

A third Israelite judge was Samson, a man of tremendous physical strength, about whom many stories have been told. Samson had to face far more powerful enemies than any of the Canaanite tribes. These were the Philistines, who came from an entirely different stock, and had settled along the coast of the Mediterranean Sea. They had built for themselves five cities, each city under its own ruler; but in times of war the armies of the five cities fought as one. The Philistines were constantly making raids inland from the plains of the coast. Their soldiers were well armed, with bronze swords and spears; and some of them, who were gigantically tall and strong, were unbeatable in single combat. When the Philistines captured a city they plundered it and left it in ruins before passing on. All the Canaanite tribes feared them, especially the tribes of Israel; for the Philistines' eastern border ran alongside Israelite land.

If the Israelites had banded together they might have resisted the Philistine advance; but at this time they lacked a leader to unite them. Samson, with his great strength and courage, slew many Philistines; but he was not a leader like Deborah or Gideon, for he had not their faith or their influence over the people. Samson had married a beautiful Philistine woman named Delilah; and the Philistines, who knew that as long as he was free he would be a danger to them, persuaded Delilah to betray him. They captured and bound him, put out both his eyes, and forced him to labour as a slave. According to the Bible story, Samson's last act showed both faith and bravery. On the feast-day of the Philistine god Dagon he was brought into the temple so that the worshippers who thronged it that day could mock at him. He was old, defeated and blind, and his physical strength had long since left him; but, stung by the mockery of his enemies and by their worship of false gods, he "called unto the Lord, and said, O Lord God, remember me, I pray thee, and strengthen me, I pray thee, only this once, O God, that I may be at once avenged of the Philistines for my two eyes. And Samson took hold of the two middle pillars upon which the house stood, and on which it was borne up, of the one with his right hand and of the other with his left. And Samson said, Let me die with the Philistines. And he bowed himself with all his might; and the house fell upon the lords, and upon all the people that were therein. So the dead which he slew at his death were more than they which he slew in his life."

There are many acts of cruelty and revenge in the stories of the Judges; but the Israelites of those days believed that it was God's will that they should take vengeance on a defeated enemy. They believed, too, in order to honour God, that when they won a victory they should destroy enemy cities and everything in them. It took them a long time to learn that death and destruction were not pleasing to God.

Each Judge, as we have seen, was the leader only of his own tribe. But one man saw how important it was for the tribes to be united. His name was Samuel and he was by far the greatest of the Judges. He lived about 1050 B.C., and he was both a priest and a prophet—an inspired teacher of the word of God.

Some time before Samuel's birth the Israelites had built a temple for the Ark at a place called Shiloh in Ephraim. They had appointed a high priest with assistant priests under him; and once a year people from all over the country came to Shiloh to pray in the temple and offer sacrifices to God. According to the Bible, a woman named Hannah, who longed for a child but had been childless for many years, prayed at Shiloh for the birth of a son, and she made a vow that, if her prayer was answered, she would give up the child to the service of God.

In due course Hannah gave birth to a son and called him Samuel. As soon as he was old enough to leave his parents Hannah brought him to Shiloh and handed him over to the care of the high priest. Though Hannah now had other children she must have missed Samuel keenly; for in the future she saw him only once a year when she came to the temple to pray; and each year she brought him a new coat which she had made.

Samuel inherited his mother's deep religious feelings, and was quite happy to be brought up in the temple and be trained as a priest. He was still very young, we are told, when he first heard the word of God and knew that he must be a prophet. But his life in the temple was brought to a violent end by the Philistines, who had been extending their strip of land northwards. At the most northerly point of the Philistine land was a place called Aphek; and to the east of Aphek was the road which led to the mountainous country where the Israelites had settled. At the mountains' edge was a place called Ebenezer; and, says the Bible, the Israelites "went out against the Philistines to battle, and pitched beside Eben-ezer: and the Philistines pitched in Aphek". In the first battle which took place the Philistines were the victors. The Israelites hurriedly sent to Shiloh for the Ark, for they imagined that if they carried it into battle with them God would give them the victory. Nothing of the sort happened. In a second battle the Israelites were completely routed. The Philistines captured the Ark (they later returned it to the Israelites); and they went on to destroy Shiloh and the temple. Other places in the hills shared the fate of Shiloh; and in recent years archaeologists have found signs of their destruction. At Seilun (which was most probably the Biblical Shiloh) archaeologists made important finds. They were not certain if the ruins they found were those of the ancient temple; but they proved without any doubt that people had lived there between about 1200 and 1000 B.C., and that the city had been destroyed during that period.

These years formed the first part of what is known as the Iron Age; and the Philistines, whose victory had given them the mastery of the hill country, had also mastered the art of working in iron and traded in iron goods. The Israelites wanted iron for their farming tools, for nails for the building of houses, and for weapons; but the Philistines refused to tell them how it was smelted. They went on to show their power over the people they had defeated by forbidding them to employ iron workers. This meant that the Israelites could not make iron weapons, and when they wanted their farm implements sharpened they had to take them humbly to Philistine smiths.

After the destruction of Shiloh Samuel was without a home. The Bible does not say how he spent the years of his early manhood, for when we next hear of him he is middle-aged. By this time he had settled in Ramah, to the south of ruined Shiloh. He was seldom at Ramah for long, but journeyed from place to place, judging—or advising—the people who flocked to him for help, settling their disputes, preaching God's word to them, and offering sacrifices. Samuel was certainly the most important man in the country. He did his utmost to strengthen the people's faith that God would not allow them to become slaves of the Philistines; and he probably encouraged them to launch a fresh attack.

Although the Philistines had overrun the Israelite country they had not conquered it completely, but there was always a danger that they would do so. There seemed only one way to meet the danger, and that was to unite the tribes under a leader who could make a nation of them, a king who would inspire them to resist.

The Bible gives two different accounts of this happening. In the first version—which is probably the more correct—we are told that the Israelites were wise to ask for a king who would rule with God's consent, and we are also told that God Himself had chosen the man. In the second version we learn that Samuel was bitterly disappointed. God, he told the Israelites, was their king, and they needed no earthly substitute.

Although we do not know exactly what happened we do know that the Israelites *were* given a king. His name was Saul, and he belonged to the tribe of Benjamin; but, as usual, there is more than one account in the Bible of how he was chosen. Saul, a very tall and fine-looking young man, was the son of a land-owner named Kish who lived in Gibeah, a hill town to the north of the city of Jerusalem. In one of the Bible stories Saul was searching for some of his father's asses which had strayed from his land. He had heard that Samuel was an exceedingly wise man and could foretell the future, and so he decided to ask him if he knew where the animals might be found. When Samuel, who had been warned by God to expect Israel's future king, saw Saul, he recognised him at once. He told Saul that he need not worry about the asses, which had already been found; and, after they had talked for some time, Samuel "took a vial of oil and poured it upon his head, and kissed him, and said, Is it not because the Lord hath anointed thee to be captain over his inheritance?" Samuel told Saul that after he had been anointed he would be a changed man, for the spirit of God would be on him. The ceremony of anointing—pouring oil on the head of a king—has come down to us through the centuries; and in England, when Queen Elizabeth II was crowned Queen in 1952 her head, like Saul's, was anointed with oil.

Another Bible story says that Saul was picked by chance. Samuel took a number of clay tablets with the name of one of the tribes inscribed on each. From these, without looking, he picked the tribe of Benjamin. Then, in the same way, he chose the name of Saul from clay tablets inscribed with the names of the men of Benjamin, and proclaimed him king. We learn from the Bible that after Saul had been anointed he went back to his home in Gibeah and lived quietly until something happened which showed him how badly the people needed a leader. The men of Jabesh-Gilead across the Jordan were being besieged by the Ammonites, another of the Canaanite tribes; and Saul, to whom the people sent for help, gathered an army and raised the siege. After this Saul began to make plans to deal with the Philistines, Israel's chief enemy. There was bitter fighting between them, and it went on for many years.

During these years Saul's children had grown up and one of his sons, Jonathan, a brave and brilliant young man, was helping his father. Once, the Bible tells us, Jonathan planned a surprise attack on the enemy. He "said unto the young man that bare his armour, Come, and let us go over to the Philistines' garrison, that is on the other side. But he told not his father." Saul and his army were in camp on the outskirts of Gibeah; and, north-east across the valley, the Philistines had occupied Michmash, a village perched on a rocky point of land. "And between the passages* by which Jonathan sought to go over unto the Philistines' garrison", the Bible account goes on, "there was a sharp rock on the one side, and a sharp rock on the other side; and the name of the one was Bozez, and the name of the other Seneh. The forefront of the one was situate northward over against Michmash, and the other southward over against Gibeah." Jonathan and his armour-bearer found the narrow passage; they crept through it, and clambered unseen up to the village of Michmash. Then they attacked. The Philistines, caught off guard, imagined that Saul's whole army was behind Jonathan. They panicked and did not know which way to turn. "And they fell before Jonathan; and his armour-bearer slew after him. And that first slaughter . . . was about twenty men, within as it were an half acre of land, which a yoke of oxen might plow." Saul's watchmen, gazing across the valley, saw the confusion and ran to tell the king. Then Saul mustered his men and led them in to the attack. The Philistines were completely routed; and so—as the Israelites believed whenever they won a victory "the Lord delivered Israel that day".

Many centuries later there was a strange sequel to the story of the battle of Michmash. In the world war of 1914-1918 Britain and her allies were fighting against Germany and *her* allies. In Palestine, which was then part of the Turkish Empire, there was a British campaign against the Turks, who were among Germany's allies. Late one evening a British major was reading his Bible by the light of a candle, searching for a name in the Book of Samuel. His brigade had been ordered to capture a village which stood on a rocky point on the far side of a deep valley; and the name of the village was Michmash. Suddenly he found it; and he read with excitement the account of how Jonathan had tricked the Philistines

* The mountain pass.

into thinking that he and his armour-bearer were part of an army. What had been done once, thought the major, might be done again. He woke his commanding officer; the two men read the account; and the commanding officer decided to send a patrol to spy out the position. The patrol found the ancient pass, which was guarded only by a few Turkish soldiers, and noticed that it led past two rocky crags—the Bozez and the Seneh of the Bible. Above, stood the village of Michmash; and nearby, clearly visible in the moonlight, was a small flat piece of land—the half-acre of the Bible. When the patrol reported back to the commanding officer he changed his plan of attack. He had meant to send the whole brigade across the valley. Instead, he sent a single company through the pass under cover of darkness. The Turks guarding the pass were quickly overpowered. The British soldiers clambered up the rocks to capture Michmash; and before sunrise they had taken up their position on the flat piece of land.

True stories like this help to make Bible descriptions real to us, for we know that the events really happened. The Bible goes on to relate how, after the defeat of the Philistines at Michmash, Saul and his army continued the war. "And there was sore war against the Philistines all the days of Saul." All the same, although the Philistines still did a great deal of damage, they had lost their former power over the Israelites and they did not regain it. And at some time during Saul's reign they were forced to hand over the secret of iron-smelting, and this meant that the Israelites could make their own iron weapons.

Saul did not fight with a very large army, but his men were carefully chosen for their courage and coolness in battle. "When Saul saw any strong man," says the Bible, "or any valiant man, he took him unto him." The most famous recruit to his army was a young man from Bethlehem in Judah, whose name was David.

CHAPTER V

DAVID, ISRAEL'S GREATEST KING

As HAPPENS SO often in the Bible, there are two different accounts of the meeting of Saul and David. During the first years of his reign Saul looked for help and advice to Samuel, who was always ready to advise him. Since he had been anointed king Saul had become far more religious than he had been as a young man; but one day Samuel came to him and accused him of disobeying God's commands. In one Bible story Saul is said to have neglected to offer the correct animal sacrifices to God before a battle. In another, he is said to have spared the life of Agag, the defeated king of the Amalekites, whom Samuel believed God had decreed must die. For one reason or another Samuel quarrelled with Saul. He warned him that God would not allow his son to succeed him as king; and he departed, refusing to see Saul again. And Saul, who admired Samuel and counted on his advice, became moody and depressed because he had offended the old prophet and, worse still, believed that he had angered God. The people, who loved their king and looked up to him, longed to rescue him from the dark moods in which by now he passed much of his time.

According to one of the Bible stories Saul, who enjoyed listening to music, asked for a musician to come and play a stringed instrument called a lyre to him, for he thought the sound might help to lift his sadness from him. His courtiers consulted together and came to the conclusion that the finest musician in the country was David, the son of Jesse of Bethlehem. So they sent for David, who was "a mighty valiant man, and a man of war", as well as a musician and a devout worshipper of God. And David played so beautifully to Saul that for a time the king forgot his melancholy.

In the second story we are told that David was only a young shepherd boy, who tended his father's flocks. He was sent by his father to take food to his elder brothers who were serving in Saul's army; and when he reached the camp he learned that the Philistine army was drawn up in battle order across the valley. The Philistines had decided not to risk fighting in the ordinary way, but in another way which was quite usual at the time. They had chosen a champion, a gigantic, heavily armed warrior named Goliath; and when David arrived Goliath was marching up and down before the Israelite camp, shouting a challenge to single combat. He would fight any Israelite warrior who took up his challenge, he cried. Whichever of them won could claim the victory for his own side, and the defeated army would become slaves of the victors.

Not a single Israelite came forward, for Goliath was a terrifying figure and towered over them all. "He had an helmet of brass upon his head", says the Bible, "and he was armed with a coat of mail; and the weight of the coat was five thousand shekels of brass. And he had greaves of brass upon his legs. . . . And the staff of his spear was like a weaver's beam; and his spear's head weighed six hundred shekels of iron: and one bearing a shield went before him." Five thousand shekels is more than 200 pounds, and 600 shekels over 24 pounds; so Goliath, if the story is true, must have been enormously strong to carry such a heavy weight.

The boy David felt no fear at all, and he told the soldiers that he would fight Goliath. This news was taken to Saul. The king sent for David, and when he saw that he was young and unarmed he tried to persuade him not to fight. "Thou art not able to go against this Philistine to fight with him," he said, "for thou art but a youth, and he a man of war from his youth." But David explained that although he was young he was very strong; and that when a lion or a bear attacked his father's sheep he was able to kill them quite easily. The "Philistine shall be as one of them," he said, "seeing he hath defied the armies of the living God." When Saul saw that David was determined to fight he clothed him in his own armour and offered him his own sword. But the armour was so heavy that the boy could not move in it. He took it off, and gave the king back his sword; and he went out to meet Goliath armed only with his shepherd's staff and a sling. A sling is a leather bag, with two thongs (strips of leather), which is whirled around the head and then one thong released, causing the ammunition, a stone, to fly out. And we are told that, as he went, David picked up five smooth pebbles from a brook.

"Am I a dog", bellowed Goliath when he saw the boy, "that thou comest to me with staves! . . . Come to me, and I will give thy flesh unto the fowls of the air, and to the beasts of the field. Then David said to the Philistine, Thou comest to me with a sword, and with a spear, and with a shield; but I come to thee in the name of the Lord of hosts, the God of the armies of Israel, whom thou hast defied."

So saying, David ran towards the battle-line of the Philistines to meet his foe. When he was within shooting distance he paused and calmly fitted a stone into his sling. He slung it; the stone struck the Philistine full on the forehead, and he fell stunned to the ground. David ran up to him, pulled the giant's sword from its sheath, and killed him as he lay on the ground unconscious. When the Israelites saw what had happened they gave a mighty shout; the Philistines turned and fled, and the triumphant Israelites followed in pursuit.

David, we know, joined Saul's army after the rout of the Philistines, and he became a warrior hero. Saul was so fond of him that he gave him one of his daughters, Michal, in marriage;

and there was a very close friendship between David and Saul's son Jonathan. We are told that David often played the lyre to the king in an effort to rouse him from the dark moods which became more frequent as he grew older; but he was not always successful. David must have fitted words of prayer and praise to God to the music he played. Because of this, the men who wrote his story in the Bible thought that he wrote a great many of the psalms, which are a collection of prayers, petitions and songs of praise and thankfulness. The book of Psalms is sometimes called "The Psalms of David"; but although David may well have written some of them, most were written by other writers who lived after him.

At first the friendship between Saul and his family and David brought them all much happiness; but unfortunately Saul grew jealous of his son-in-law, who had become very popular with the people. We are told that when the king returned victorious from battle he was always greeted by a band of women who sang his praises; but now, when they sang, "Saul hath slain his thousands", they added, "and David his ten thousands." This made Saul extremely angry. "They have ascribed unto David ten thousands," he said, "and to me they have ascribed but thousands: and what can he have more but the kingdom?" From that time onwards Saul was suspicious of the younger man, for he feared that David might try and seize the kingdom. Saul need not have feared, for David was absolutely loyal; but his fears grew so strong that he made two attempts to kill David. In the end David was forced to flee for his life and go into hiding. Even so, he was not safe, for Saul, as he knew, was plotting to have him put to death.

We know today that Saul's fierce jealousy and his black moods showed that he was no longer sane. Like many people who suffer from a certain kind of madness, there were days when the darkness suddenly lifted from his mind, and once again he was his generous, noble self. And although the people feared his melancholy and his jealous rages, they continued to love him, for they remembered him as he had been in the early years of his reign. When the darkness lifted Saul realised how cruelly he was treating David; but the darkness returned and, with it, all his fears.

David by now was living the life of an outlaw, hiding in caves and woods, and never staying long in one place. He was no longer alone, for many men thought he was being unjustly treated and joined him in hiding; and as the years went by the number of David's supporters grew. Once, we are told, David could easily have killed Saul. The king was searching for David in order to kill him when he became separated from his followers. He entered a cave and, although he did not know it, David and his men were hiding in the darkness of the cave. When they saw that the king was alone, David's men urged their leader to kill him; but David refused. Instead, he came out of the shadows and spoke to Saul, begging him to believe that he would never do him any harm. "Behold, this day," he said, "thine eyes have seen how that the Lord had delivered thee today into mine hand . . .; and some bade me kill thee: but mine eye spared thee; and I said, I will not put forth mine hand against my lord; for he is the Lord's anointed. . . . I have not sinned against thee; yet thou huntest my soul to take it."

When David had finished speaking the king was filled with remorse. "Saul lifted up his voice, and wept. And he said to David, Thou art more righteous than I: for thou hast rewarded me good, whereas I have rewarded thee evil. . . . And now, behold, I know well that thou shalt surely be king, and that the kingdom of Israel shall be established in thine hand. Swear now therefore unto me by the Lord, that thou wilt not cut off my seed after me, and that thou wilt not destroy my name out of my father's house. And David sware unto Saul." There is another version of this story in the Bible, and in the second version Saul appears even more contrite: "I have sinned; return, my son David: for I will no more do thee harm, because my soul was precious in thine eyes this day: behold I have played the fool, and have erred exceedingly."

At this moment Saul really meant what he said. But David knew, and so did his friend Jonathan, that Saul's black mood would return. When it came back Saul forgot that he had repented; and he continued to hunt David like an animal until, in despair, David took refuge with the Philistines; for he thought—and rightly—that Saul would not venture to seek him among his worst enemies.

By this time there were rumours in Israel that David, and not Jonathan, would succeed Saul as king when he died. Jonathan had heard the rumours; but he and David were devoted friends, and he admired David too much to wish to be king over him, and he was willing to serve David loyally. In his eagerness to kill David, Saul had been neglecting one of his most important duties—to guard Israel's frontiers against the Philistines. The Philistines, who realised what was happening, launched a full-scale attack. A grim battle was fought and was won by the Philistines; and the defeated Israelites turned and fled. When the battle was over Saul and three of his sons, Jonathan among them, lay dead. The young men had been slain fighting; but Saul, who had survived, had killed himself rather than fall into the hands of the enemy.

The triumphant Philistines seized the bodies of the dead king and his sons and hanged them from the walls of one of their cities—Beth-shan. But the men of Jabesh-Gilead had not forgotten how, when Saul first became king, he had rescued them from becoming slaves of the Ammonites. And so, "when the inhabitants of Jabesh-gilead heard of that which the Philistines had done to Saul; All the valiant men arose and went all night, and took the body of Saul and the bodies of his sons from the wall of Beth-shan, and came to Jabesh, and burnt them there. And they took their bones, and buried them under a tree at Jabesh, and fasted seven days."

When news of the disaster was brought to David, who was still in hiding, he tore his clothes as a sign of mourning. And David and all the men who were with him "mourned, and wept, and fasted until even, for Saul, and for Jonathan his son, and for the people of the Lord, and for the house of Israel; because they were fallen by the sword". Then David wrote a poem of lament for Saul and Jonathan and of praise for their valour; and he gave orders for it to be taught to the people of Judah:

"The beauty of Israel is slain upon thy high places: how are the mighty fallen!

"Saul and Jonathan were lovely and pleasant in their lives, and in their death they were not divided: they were swifter than eagles, they were stronger than lions.

"How are the mighty fallen, and the weapons of war perished!"

Israel was now without a king, but Saul had more than one son left alive; and Saul's general, Abner, named one of them— Ishbaal—king. In the meantime, the people of David's tribe— Judah—had invited him to be their king, and David had agreed. Saul and his family had lived in the north and Judah was in the south; and so the kingdom became divided, with David king in the south and Ishbaal in the north. This was not a good plan. It caused enmity between the people of the north and south and led to civil war. But after two years of strife Abner saw that Israel needed a ruler who would unite the country; and he knew that David would be a far better king than Ishbaal. And so he sent to David at his capital, Hebron, to ask him to be king; but he made it a condition that David would deal kindly with Saul's descendants. David gladly agreed to Abner's condition, for he had no wish to deal harshly with Saul's family. "So all the elders of Israel came to the king to Hebron; and King David made a league with them in Hebron before the Lord: and they anointed David king over Israel. David was thirty years old when he began to reign, and he reigned forty years."

David's reign lasted from about 1018 to 978 B.C. The new king did not forget his promise to Abner; and when he learned that Jonathan had left a young son who was a cripple, he sent for him at once. The boy, who was afraid, bowed low before the king. "Fear not," said David gently, "for I will surely shew thee kindness for Jonathan thy father's sake, and will restore thee all the land of Saul thy father;* and thou shalt eat bread at my table continuously." David did as he had promised. He gave back the dead king's possessions to the boy, and ordered Saul's servants to wait on him and till his land.

David was the greatest of Israel's kings. He believed devoutly in God. He brought the tribes together as one nation; and he gained a complete victory over the Philistines and the other enemies of Israel. He chose the capital of his kingdom with great care. If he had decided to keep Hebron as his capital or had chosen another city far to the south, he would have offended the people of the north. In the same way, he would have annoyed his own people of Judah if he had chosen a northern city. Instead, he chose a city in the very centre of the kingdom. This was the hill fortress of Jebus (or Jerusalem as it was also called), which had been held by a Canaanite tribe, the Jebusites, ever since the Israelites entered Palestine. Jebus was built on a hill, one of two hills which formed a tableland. The tableland was surrounded by valleys on the east and west, and the Jebusites, whose fortress was strongly guarded, had a good view of everything that went on below. So far no one had been able to take the fortress from them, and David probably felt that its capture would make a spectacular beginning to his reign.

The Jebusites were sure they could easily repel any attack; and they sent David a scornful message: "Except thou take away the blind and the lame," they said, "thou shalt not come in hither: thinking, David cannot come in hither." But David ordered his men to get up the gutter—or water-shaft; and he "took the stronghold" . . .

This water-shaft—or rock tunnel—solved David's problem.

* The word Father, in biblical language, is also used to mean forefather.

He must have discovered that it had been dug right into the centre of the fortress; and so, instead of laying siege to the stronghold, his men crept through the tunnel, took the defenders by surprise, and captured the city. David then made Jerusalem his capital; and the city was also called Zion, after one of the hills of the tableland on which it stood.

About a hundred years ago experts discovered how David's men had entered Jerusalem. On its eastern side, where the rocky slope descends to the Kidron Valley, there is a spring which has supplied the city with water through the centuries; and in the Hebrew Bible this spring is called Gihon, which means "bubbler". In 1867 and Englishman, Captain Charles Warren, was making sketch maps of the country and digging on one of Jerusalem's hills. There he made a most interesting discovery. He found that the early people of Jerusalem really had cut a tunnel through the rock which must have allowed them to get water from the spring of Gihon, without being seen by their enemies outside. The tunnel led the waters of the Gihon from the spot where they flowed out of the rock to a cave in the middle of the city, which formed a reservoir—or storage tank. This meant that even during a siege the people would never have been without water. Above the reservoir Captain Warren found a passage leading to a platform of rock; and he realised that the women must often have stood on this rock to lower their drinking jars into the water. Archaeologists think that the tunnel was probably used from the time of the Judges until the fortress was captured by David. Within the last few years new discoveries have been made which show that the ancient fortress was much larger than it was thought to have been, and the walls so thick that the Jebusites may have been right in thinking that nobody could break them down.

When David made Jerusalem his capital he decided that the city, which he planned to enlarge, should also be the centre of Israel's religious life. He therefore ordered the Ark of the Covenant to be brought in procession to Jerusalem, and he had a special tabernacle made for it on Zion. When all was ready and the cart

carrying the Ark came in sight, its appearance was greeted by the
king and his people playing "on harps, and on psalteries, and on
timbrels, and on cornets, and on cymbals". From his youth
David had loved music and, as we know, he was a fine musician.
The ancient music which greeted the appearance of the Ark must
have sounded something like the jazz music of modern times,
with the rhythm of the various percussion instruments. It was
certainly very lively; for we are told that the king "danced before
the Lord with all his might".

The music and dancing were a sign of joy and also of respect.
Afterwards there was a solemn ceremony. "And they brought in
the ark of the Lord, and set it in his place, in the midst of the
tabernacle that David had pitched for it: and David offered burnt
offerings and peace offerings before the Lord. And . . . David
blessed the people in the name of the Lord of hosts. And he dealt
among all the people, even among the whole multitude of Israel,
as well to the women as men, to everyone a cake of bread, and a
good piece of flesh, and a flagon of wine. So all the people
departed, every one to his house."

David did not intend to leave the Ark in a simple tent. He
planned to build for it a large and splendid temple; but, according
to the Bible, he was prevented from doing so by Nathan, the
great prophet of his reign. Nathan reminded David that the Law
of God had been safely kept in a tent for generations and should
not be moved. Then he told the king that God had decreed that
his descendants should rule after him; and David offered up a
prayer of thanksgiving for God's unfailing help: "For thou hast
confirmed to thyself thy people Israel to be a people unto thee for
ever: and thou, Lord, art become their God."

The people of Israel looked on David as their religious leader,
and also as a warrior who had made Israel strong. The Bible is so
full of stories of his conquests that it tells us very little about how
he governed the country. We are told that he was a great king;
and the loyalty of his followers in the days when he was a fugitive
shows that he was very much loved. But he had many faults; and

it is just because the Bible does not try to hide them that we can see him, not simply as a character in a book, but as a real human being. David could be kind, generous and forgiving, as he was when he refused to kill Saul when the king was in his power, and when he adopted Jonathan's crippled son and returned Saul's possessions to him. Yet, like other warriors of his day, he was cruel and merciless in war; he was quick-tempered and reckless; and there were times when he acted most unjustly. It was partly because of these faults that David was not allowed to build the Temple.

According to the custom of the day, David had many wives besides Michal, Saul's daughter. His worst act of injustice concerned one of them, Bathsheba, who was the wife of one of the officers of his army when David first saw her. The officer's name was Uriah. He was not an Israelite but a Hittite; for David had recruited a number of foreigners to his army, who served him as loyally as his own people. At the time Uriah was with a company which was besieging the city of Rabbah, then held by the Ammonites. David gave orders to the commander that Uriah should be placed in the front of the advance force; and that when Uriah had taken his place the force should retreat, leaving him at the mercy of the enemy. The commander obeyed the king's orders, and Uriah was killed, as David had known he must be. When Bathsheba had mourned for her dead husband according to custom, David married her, and, to his great delight, she had a son.

David's cruel and unjust act had angered his subjects; and the prophet Nathan warned him that his crime would not go unpunished. In order to show the king how wrong he had been, Nathan told him a story about two men. One of them, he said, was rich, with many flocks and herds. The other was so poor that he owned nothing but a single ewe lamb, which he had tamed and which ate and slept with his family. One day a traveller called on the rich man; and the rich man, who kept the laws of hospitality, invited the traveller to come in and eat. He did not want to kill any of his own sheep; and so he stole the poor man's lamb, and killed and prepared it for his guest. Then David burst out angrily: "As the Lord liveth, the man that hath done this thing shall surely die: And he shall restore the lamb fourfold, because he did this thing, and because he had no pity. And Nathan said to David, Thou art the man." The prophet also told David that because of his crime there would be strife among the members of his own family. And David, who had so many good impulses, was overcome with guilt. "I have sinned against the Lord," he cried. And Nathan told him that there was still another punishment in store for him—the death of Bathsheba's son.

There had been prophets in Israel before Nathan's time. Some of the earliest of them were rather wild men, who went about in groups trying to stir up the religious feelings of the people by dancing and music. The first prophets were known as "seers". They were thought to have been granted by God the power to see into the future so that they could help and advise the people and warn them that misery would follow crime. Samuel was a seer; and Saul went to him to enquire the whereabouts of his father's lost asses. But Samuel was also an inspired teacher; and gradually the teachings of a prophet were becoming more important than the "seeing".

The prophets were still believed to be able to foretell happenings; and so we are told in the Bible that soon after Nathan had delivered his solemn warning to David, Bathsheba's son did indeed die, to the great grief of his parents. Today, of course, nobody thinks a child should die for his father's sin; but in those days a man's children, especially his sons, were looked on as a part of him, far more so than they are today. And so the death of the child, who was part of David, was thought to be a just punishment for the guilty father. David comforted Bathsheba in her grief; and later on she had another son, Solomon, who became king after his father.

Nathan's prophecy about strife in the family also came true, perhaps because Nathan understood David very well indeed, and could see that he was making trouble for himself. David loved his children dearly, and his love made him foolish and indulgent towards them. He spoilt his sons, and gave in to all their demands; and the boys grew up to be wilful and extravagant. They were always quarrelling; they took life far too easily; and not one of them became a really great man like his father.

David's best-loved son was Absalom, a proud, ambitious young man, famous for his splendid looks and his thick and beautiful hair. Absalom was so ambitious that he planned to make himself king instead of his father. He stirred up the old strife between the men of Israel in the north and the men of Judah in the south; and he managed to make himself so popular in the north that he was able to raise an army to revolt against David. When the king learned that Absalom was leading his forces southwards against him he fled in despair from Jerusalem. He could not bear the idea of fighting against his own son; but he still had many loyal followers who loved and trusted him and would serve no one else. One of them was a foreigner, Ittai, a Gittite. When David saw that Ittai was prepared to come with him, he said to him: "Thou camest but yesterday, Should I this day make thee go up and down with us? seeing I go whither I may, return thou, and take back thy brethren: mercy and truth be with thee. And Ittai answered the king, and said, As the Lord liveth, and as my lord the king liveth, surely in what place my lord the king shall be, whether in death or life, even there also will thy servant be. And David said to Ittai, Go and pass over."

When David left Jerusalem he climbed the Mount of Olives, which rises from the Kidron Valley, to pray; for worship was offered to God on the summit. He was an old man now, broken by his son's treachery; and the Bible gives us a pathetic picture of him in his sorrow. "And David went up by the ascent of mount Olivet, and wept as he went up, and had his head covered, and he went barefoot: and all the people that was with him covered every man his head, and they went up, weeping as they went up." Afterwards David and his loyal followers crossed the Jordan; and Absalom in triumph entered Jerusalem.

David had expected Absalom to pursue him at once; but Absalom delayed; and David, who knew that he must defend himself, had time to recruit an army. He himself took no part in the fighting; and his forces defeated Absalom's. David had charged his men on no account to kill his son; but Absalom, who was riding a mule, passed under a tree and was caught by his thick hair in one of its branches. And there, in defiance of David's orders, he was killed.

News of the victory and of Absalom's death was brought to the waiting king. But David could not think of the victory, only of his dead son. "O my son Absalom my son, my son Absalom!" he mourned. "Would God I had died for thee, O Absalom, my son, my son!" He could not give way to his grief for long; for the men of Israel and Judah, united once more, begged him to return to Jerusalem. He went back and continued to rule; but the last years of his life were darkened by further strife in his own family. One of his other sons proclaimed himself king; and David, who by that time was dying, roused himself to name Solomon as his heir. Before he died he urged Solomon never to fail in his worship of God or to forget His commandments.

During Solomon's reign the splendid Temple which David had planned was built; and one of the old Hebrew legends explains how this great house of prayer reflected honour on David. When the Ark was carried into the Temple it was reverently placed in the farthest corner, behind a curtain. Immediately the Ark had been set down the door shut itself firmly, and nobody could open it. Solomon prayed earnestly to God to open the door; but it remained closed until he said these words: "Remember the good deeds of David, thy servant." When Solomon had finished speaking the door swung open; and everybody—even David's enemies—felt sure that the sins he had committed in his lifetime had been forgiven.

CHAPTER VI

SOLOMON WEAKENS THE KINGDOM

IN JANUARY, 1964, the Pope, head of the Roman Catholic Church, who was on a pilgrimage to the Holy Places of the New Testament, was welcomed into the Jewish State of Israel by the President, Israel's head of state. The two men met at Megiddo in the valley of Jezreel (it is also called the valley of Esdraelon) which in Biblical times had been a fortress. The pass of Megiddo, on the main highway linking Syria with Egypt, was used for centuries by armies and caravans of traders; and in the historic valley of Jezreel Deborah and Barak led the Hebrews to victory against the Canaanites.

Archaeologists believe that the fortress of Megiddo was destroyed about 1150 B.C. (in the time of the Judges) and was rebuilt about fifty years later. During King Solomon's lifetime (he reigned from about 976 to 936 B.C.) Megiddo must have flourished. In about 1930 two American archaeologists, P. L. O. Guy and Gordon Loud, came to the conclusion that the stumps of rows of pillars which had been discovered at Megiddo were part of some huge stables and had once been used to divide the stalls from one another. According to the Bible, Solomon had vast numbers of horses, horsemen and chariots; and at Megiddo chariot sheds and barracks for grooms were also found. Although Megiddo is not mentioned in the Bible as one of the places where Solomon stabled his horses, it *is* mentioned as one of the districts into which he divided his kingdom; and archaeologists think that at least some of the buildings date from Solomon's reign.

In 1937, and again in 1940, another American expedition, led this time by Professor Nelson Glueck, made some further exciting discoveries. The expedition explored the Wadi el-Arabah (the Valley of the Desert), the sandy region in the far south of Palestine between the Dead Sea and the Red Sea, which had once been occupied by the Edomites who had been conquered by David. Professor Glueck, who studied the whole valley and the country which lies to the east and west of it, discovered that copper and iron had been mined there in ancient times; and he found the remains of a number of simple furnaces in which the first stage of smelting the metal had been carried out. He also found the remains of walls, and of other things, copper fish-hooks and baked clay pottery among them. Archaeologists can generally tell the date of a pot by its pattern and shape; and the Arabah pottery, they decided, belonged to the Early Iron Age. As we saw, it was during the Early Iron Age that the Philistines, who knew how to work iron, had been forced to give up the secret to David; and so the iron was probably mined and worked by the Israelites during David's reign or soon after.

The walls and other remains discovered by Professor Glueck also belonged to the Early Iron Age, which showed that they had once formed part of a settlement (or town). At first he could not make out why people had chosen to live in such a very awkward spot; for the settlement was some way from the nearest supply of fresh water, and it stood right in the path of hot, sand-carrying winds from the north. He believed that he had solved this problem when he found the remains of what appeared to be an enormous plant for the smelting of copper and iron. In this area he found traces of what seemed to be furnace rooms with flues (or openings) placed in such a way as to make full use of the winds from the north to fan the fires. If this were so, then metal from the Arabah mines would have been taken after its first rough smelting to be finished in the main smelting plant. Much of the metal would then have been sent by ship to southern Arabia and eastern Africa; and Professor Glueck found traces which proved to him that ship-building had also been carried on in the settlement. It is most probable that the settlement was the Biblical town of Ezion-Geber; for we are told that "King Solomon made a navy of ships in Ezion-geber, which is beside Eloth, on the shore of the Red Sea, in the land of Edom." Since Professor Glueck explored the district other expeditions have visited it and further excavations are being carried out.

The copper used for the pillars and sacred vessels in the magnificent Temple which Solomon built at Jerusalem came from Ezion-Geber. And the Bible tells us that after the Ark had been brought in procession to the Temple from the simple tabernacle in which it had been kept during David's reign, Solomon, like his father before him, blessed the people and offered sacrifices to God.

Solomon was a very different sort of man from David. He was a stately, dignified king, a man who amassed great wealth. We do not get from the Bible as clear a picture of Solomon as we do of the very human David. At the beginning of Solomon's reign, we are told, God appeared to the king in a dream, saying, "Ask what I shall give thee." Solomon asked for "an understanding heart" to govern his people; and God was so pleased with his request that He gave him honour and riches as well.

King Solomon, then, was known for his wisdom. He is called in the Bible "Solomon, the wise"; and the Book of Proverbs—or wise sayings—is called after him, *The Proverbs of Solomon*. He was certainly a good judge of people, and we are told that he settled many disputes. The story of how he settled one of these disputes is famous. Two women came before him with a difficult problem. They lived in the same house; and each of them had recently given birth to a son. The mother of the elder baby told the king that the younger one had died during the night, and that while she and her own baby slept, the mother of the dead child had exchanged the babies, leaving her with a dead child. The second woman denied that she had done any such thing, and claimed that the living child was hers. "Then said the king, The one saith, This is my son that liveth, and thy son is the dead; and the other saith, Nay; but thy son is the dead, and my son is the living. . . . And the king said, Divide the living child in two, and give half to the one, and half to the other." Then the first woman cried out, "O my lord, give her the living child, and in no wise slay it. But the other said, Let it be neither mine nor thine, but divide it." Then Solomon ordered the living child to be given to the first woman, for "she is the mother thereof". The king had guessed correctly; for he knew that the real mother would sooner her child was brought up by another woman than that it should die.

There are many other stories in the Bible about Solomon's wisdom and his importance. We are told that his fame spread far and wide, as far as the land of Sheba in the south of the Arabian Peninsula. "And when the queen of Sheba heard of the fame of Solomon concerning the name of the Lord, she came to prove him with hard questions. And she came to Jerusalem with a very great train, with camels that bare spices, and very much gold, and precious stones: and when she was come to Solomon, she communed with him of all that was in her heart. And Solomon told her all her questions: there was not any thing hid from the king, which he told her not." The queen of Sheba was deeply impressed by all that she had seen and heard. "Blessed be the Lord thy God, which delighted in thee, to set thee on the throne of Israel," she cried. . . . "And she gave the king an hundred and twenty talents of gold, and of spices very great store, and precious stones: there came no more such abundance of spices as these which the queen of Sheba gave to King Solomon."

It is probable that the queen of Sheba wanted Israel to trade in various goods with her country. Israel needed spices; and Sheba may have needed copper and iron from Ezion-Geber. If the queen of Sheba asked Solomon to sign a trade agreement with her, he must have done so; for we are told that before she departed for her own country he gave her "all her desire, whatsoever she asked, beside that which Solomon gave her of his royal bounty."

Solomon was wise enough to see that trade with other countries would help to make Israel prosperous. The sea voyage from Ezion-Geber to the distant countries of southern Arabia and back took three years; but trade by land was being made much simpler and swifter by the use, as a pack animal, of the tireless, fast-moving camel instead of the ass. And during Solomon's long reign Israel prospered and was at peace with her neighbours.

The king was a devout worshipper of God; and in the Temple which he had built and dedicated he offered regular sacrifices, according to the customs of his day. But, although he was a religious man and famous for his wisdom, in some ways he was most unwise. In order to pay the foreigners who helped to build the Temple and his palaces, fortresses and stables, he taxed his own people heavily. They had to pay in grain from their crops, animals from their flocks and herds; and sometimes he forced them to work without any reward. Even so, Solomon could not pay all his debts to the foreign builders; and so in the end he had to give away some of Israel's towns in exchange for their services. This made his own people very angry. Some of them revolted against him; but the revolt was soon put down, and the leader—a man named Jeroboam—fled to Egypt for safety.

Solomon also showed his lack of wisdom in his treatment of his many foreign wives. His chief wife was an Egyptian princess; and among the others were women from many different countries and tribes. David had also married foreign wives; and foreigners had served loyally in his army. David had never allowed the influence of foreigners to become too strong; but Solomon, although he always worshipped God himself, built altars and chapels so that his wives could worship the gods of their own countries, and allowed their pagan priests to enter Israel.

All this led to a weakening of Israel's faith and power; and
Solomon's death was followed by strife and civil war between the
men of Israel and Judah. Solomon was succeeded as king by his
son, Rehoboam, who was far more foolish in his dealings with
his people than Solomon. When they begged him to lighten the
burden of taxes which Solomon had imposed he replied scornfully
that in future their burden would be heavier than ever. This made
the people of the north so angry that they decided to appoint a
king of their own and have nothing more to do with Rehoboam.
They chose Jeroboam, who had led the revolt against Solomon.

Rehoboam was deposed and Jeroboam made king at Shechem,
a city some thirty miles north of Jerusalem. Shechem was the first
place in Palestine mentioned in the Bible, which relates that
Abraham encamped there and built an altar to the Lord. As the
years went by Shechem grew in prosperity as the capital of a city
state. In recent years—between 1956 and 1964—an American
archaeological expedition unearthed the ruins of the city and
discovered traces of huge fortifications and gates.

Jeroboam made Shechem his capital for a time; but with his
choice as king the northern kingdom, Israel (or Ephraim as it was
sometimes called) separated itself from Judah, where Rehoboam
continued to rule. Israel was the larger and more important of the
two kingdoms because it contained ten of the twelve tribes; while
the southern kingdom had only two tribes, Judah and Benjamin,
whose people remained loyal to a descendant of David.

In one way Judah was still the centre of all the tribes. Jerusalem,
the capital, was in Judah; and in Jerusalem was the Temple to
which the people from the north as well as the south came to
worship on festival days. This worried Jeroboam, who feared that
his people might desert him. He therefore set up two shrines in
Israel where the people could worship God, one at Dan and one at
Beth-el; and in each shrine he placed the golden image of a bull.

Jeroboam on the whole was a wise and sensible king; but he
made a great mistake when he opened these shrines. He intended
the golden bulls simply to stand for the idea of God; and he did

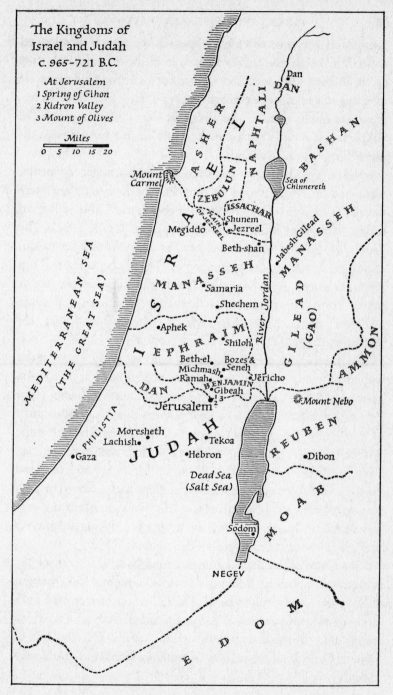

The Kingdoms of
Israel and Judah
C. 965-721 B.C.

At Jerusalem
1 Spring of Gihon
2 Kidron Valley
3 Mount of Olives

Miles
0 5 10 15 20

Dan
DAN

ASHER

ZEBULUN

NAPHTALI

BASHAN

Sea of
Chinnereth

Mount
Carmel

ISSACHAR
Shunem
Jezreel
Megiddo
PLAIN OF JEZREEL

Beth-shan

Jabesh-Gilead

I S R A E L

MANASSEH

MANASSEH
Samaria

Shechem

River Jordan

GILEAD
(GAO)

AMMON

Aphek

E P H R A I M
Shiloh

Beth-el
Michmash
Ramah
DAN

Bozes &
Seneh
BENJAMIN
Gibeah
Jericho

Mount Nebo

Jerusalem
3

MEDITERRANEAN SEA
(THE GREAT SEA)

PHILISTIA

Moresheth
Lachish
Gaza

J U D A H

Tekoa
Hebron

Dead Sea
(Salt Sea)

REUBEN

Dibon

M O A B

Sodom

NEGEV

E D O M

D

not mean the people to worship them as the pagans worshipped idols. But the Israelites were forbidden in their Commandments to set up any likeness of God; and although at the time the exact meaning of a likeness—or image—may not have been understood, the golden bulls were so like idols that after a while some of the people began to worship them. And this led to a further weakening of Israel's religious faith.

Israel and Judah, now separate and independent countries, were not nearly as strong as they had been when they were united. They were often at war with one another, although from time to time they joined together to face an outside attack. The people of Judah (Judeans, or Jews as they were later called) remained loyal to the memory of David, and their kings were descended from him. In Israel, the kingship no longer passed from father to son as a matter of course; and some of Israel's kings were army officers who seized power for themselves.

The most able of Israel's kings was an army commander named Omri, who ruled from about 882 to 871 B.C. and did a great deal to make Israel strong again. During Omri's reign Palestine was threatened by a new power—Assyria. The country of Assyria lay along the upper part of the Tigris River; but the Assyrians, who were a Semitic people like the Israelites, had already made themselves overlords of Mesopotamia, the land between the Tigris and the Euphrates. Now they planned to push westwards across the Euphrates towards Syria (or Aram as it was called) and Palestine, for they were bent on making themselves masters of the middle eastern world.

King Omri of Israel thought that he might be able to check the invading Assyrians by building a fortified city; and so he bought a hill in the Samarian highlands. The hill was protected by a half-circle of mountains; and it had a spring of fresh water, which meant that it could withstand a long siege. On the hill of Samaria Omri built the fortress of Samaria, which was also Israel's
. capital.

The Assyrians did not march against Israel during Omri's litetime; and Omri strengthened the country by subduing the kingdom of Moab which lay to the east of the Salt (or Dead) Sea. He was certainly respected as a king; for a hundred years after his family had ceased to reign the Assyrians still spoke of Israel as "the house of Omri". And he was powerful enough to be able to arrange a marriage for his son, Ahab, with a princess from the important neighbouring kingdom of Phoenicia, which extended along the eastern coast of the Mediterranean.

Although Omri did much for his country the Bible says of him that he "wrought evil in the eyes of the Lord, and did worse than all that were before him". The writers of the two books of Kings, who described Omri and many of the other kings as doing evil, did so for their own reasons. They were not interested in what a king did for his country. They wanted to show that any king who neglected to worship God in what *they* considered the right and proper way was a wicked man. But we have to remember that these writers lived about two hundred and fifty years after Omri; and they accused him and other kings of breaking religious laws which were not even thought of when they were alive.

The writers did more than this. They wrote as though their ideas were God's ideas, spoken to the people by God's prophets. When a new king seized power he often tried to make himself secure by killing the family of the king he had succeeded; and the writers claimed that God, through the prophets, approved of the murders as a just punishment for people who had failed to worship Him in the right way.

Ahab, Omri's son, had some good points, which are scarcely mentioned in the books of Kings; but he also had some very bad points, and we hear a great deal about them. He was a weaker character than his favourite wife Jezebel, the Phoenician princess. Jezebel was a firm believer in Melkart, the idol—or baal—worshipped by her people; and she brought with her from Phoenicia several hundred priests and prophets. Solomon, as we saw, allowed his foreign wives to bring their priests with them; but since his death this habit had stopped in Israel. Solomon's wives had not tried to convert the Israelites to the worship of their gods; but Jezebel was determined to force her religion on them. When Israel's prophets and priests attempted to stop her, she had them hunted down and persecuted. Ahab allowed his strong-willed wife to do what she liked. For a time he, too, seems to have worshipped Melkart, although later he returned to the worship of God. The people, worried and frightened by what was happening, tried to combine the two religions, worshipping both God and the baal.

While Jezebel and her priests were seeking to gain complete religious mastery in Israel the prophet Elijah, one of the greatest men of Biblical times, came forward to stop them. Elijah and the prophets who came after him were strong in the belief that God had entrusted them with a message which they must deliver whatever the cost. People still consulted the prophets about future happenings, such as the result of a battle which had not yet taken place. But the importance of the prophets was in their teaching; and this they gave fearlessly, even though they risked death not once but many times.

Elijah came to the court of Ahab and Jezebel from his home in Gilead on the edge of the wilderness beyond the Jordan. Physically he was very strong, for he was used to a rough and comfortless life and could exist on very little food. His clothes were rough, too; for we are told that "he wore a garment of haircloth, with a girdle of leather about his loins".

Elijah's task was to bring the people of Israel, who wavered between loyalty to God and to Jezebel's baal, back to the worship of God. To do this he set out to prove that God, who was the true God, was all-powerful and that Melkart was a useless image. Jezebel hated and feared him; but Ahab, who also feared him, allowed him to speak freely.

When the prophet first confronted the king he predicted a period of drought which God alone could end. Then he disappeared, and returned only when the long drought had caused famine and misery in the land. "Art thou he that troubleth Israel?" demanded Ahab when he saw Elijah once again. To this the prophet replied: "I have not troubled Israel; but thou, and thy father's house, in that ye have forsaken the commandments of the Lord, and thou hast followed Baalim." Elijah then called for a test between the power of God and the power of Melkart. He demanded that all Jezebel's priests and prophets should assemble on Mount Carmel at the north-west tip of Israel's mountain range; and he ordered everybody to follow them to the mountains. "How long halt ye between two opinions?" he asked the people: by this he meant, how long would they try to get the best of both worlds by worshipping God and Melkart at the same time. "If the Lord be God, follow him" cried Elijah; "but if Baal, then follow him. And the people answered him not a word." But they followed Elijah and the priests and prophets of Melkart to the summit of Mount Carmel. There two bulls were slaughtered; and one was cut up and placed on a pile of wood put together by the pagans. The wood was not set alight; but Elijah told the pagans to ask their god to send fire to burn it. For hours on end they called on their god; but nothing happened, not even when they raved and cut themselves with swords and lances, after one of their barbaric customs.

Then "Elijah said unto all the people, Come near unto me. And all the people came near unto him." He took twelve stones —the number of the tribes—and built an altar with them. He laid the pieces of the second bull on wood which he had placed on the altar, and dug a deep trench around it; and he ordered water to be poured over the altar so that it soaked the dead animal and filled the trench. When this had been done, "Elijah the prophet came near, and said, Lord God of Abraham, Isaac, and of Israel, let it be known this day that thou art God in Israel, and that I am thy servant, and that I have done all these things at thy word. Hear me, O Lord, hear me, that this people may know that thou art the Lord God, and that thou hast turned their heart back again.

Then the fire of the Lord fell, and consumed the burnt sacrifice, and the wood, and the stones, and the dust, and licked up the water that was in the trench. And when all the people saw it, they fell on their faces: and they said, The Lord, he is the God; the Lord, he is the God." Elijah then ordered the people to seize the priests and prophets of the baal; and all the pagans were dragged down into the valley and killed.

Elijah then climbed Mount Carmel again; "and he cast himself down upon the earth, and put his face between his knees". And he sent the servant who was with him to look out over the sea for signs of rain. The servant saw nothing; but Elijah sent him back to look seven times. At the seventh time the servant reported, "Behold, there ariseth a little cloud out of the sea like a man's hand." And Elijah said to his servant, "Go up, say unto Ahab, Prepare thy chariot and get thee down, that the rain stop thee not. And it came to pass in the meanwhile, that the heaven was black with clouds and wind, and there was a great rain. And Ahab rode, and went to Jezreel. And the hand of the Lord was on Elijah; and he girded up his loins, and ran before Ahab to the entrance of Jezreel."

There are many other stories in the Bible which show Elijah's faith and the great efforts he made to bring the people back to the worship of God. He did not write down his message, as the later prophets were to do. Stories of his deeds were handed down from father to son, and in the retelling of miraculous happenings much was probably added which was not strictly true. The people who told and retold the stories were quite sure that it was at God's command that the priests and prophets of the baal had been slaughtered; for the time had not yet come when they could understand the meaning of mercy. But two things are absolutely clear in the stories about Elijah. One is his own faith; the other is his courage, even when he risked a violent death.

After the killing of the prophets of the baal, we are told, Jezebel's hatred of Elijah reached such a pitch that she threatened to take his life. He went into hiding; but the voice of God—or the voice of his own conscience—would not let him rest; and so once more he returned to defy Ahab and his furious queen. This time he was fighting against cruelty and injustice.

Ahab, we are told, had wanted to enlarge the grounds of his palace by adding a neighbouring vineyard to it, and had offered Naboth, the owner, a fair price. But Naboth, who had inherited the ground from his father, refused to sell. Naboth's refusal angered Ahab, but there seemed to him to be nothing he could do about it. He told Jezebel, and the wily queen advised him to leave things to her. She then wrote letters in the king's name ordering false charges of treason to be brought against Naboth. These orders were obeyed; and the innocent Naboth was stoned to death. The triumphant Jezebel told her husband that he was now free to take possession of the vineyard; and he did so.

There was absolutely no excuse for what Jezebel had done, and no excuse for Ahab, who had allowed her to do what she liked. Elijah returned to warn Ahab that as a punishment he and Jezebel would both die violently, and that their whole family would be wiped out.

Yet Ahab, despite his weakness, showed wisdom and strength in the defence of his country. When Benhadad, the king of Syria attacked Samaria he was defeated by Ahab's forces. After the battle, instead of putting the defeated king to death as he might have done, Ahab made a friend and an ally of him. And so, when the king of Assyria—Shalmaneser III—led his army across the Euphrates on its westward march he was met by a powerful alliance of kings, the kings of Israel and Syria among them; and the records of Shalmaneser show that "Ahab the Israelite" had the strongest force. Shalmaneser's advance was checked for the time being at Qarqar on the River Orontes, where a battle was fought in 853.

The writers of the books of Kings say nothing about the check to Shalmaneser's advance. They mention Ahab's alliance with

Benhadad of Syria; but they add that he was rebuked for weakness in making the alliance by one of the prophets. Perhaps Ahab, who had shown mercy to the king of Syria, was worried by the rebuke, which may have helped to set many of his own people against him. In any event, the alliance with Syria did not last very long; and when it came to an end Ahab joined forces with Jehoshaphat, king of Judah, against Syria. Jehoshaphat, who ruled from about 873 to 849 B.C., was an able king. He strengthened his country by building a number of fortified cities; but he made an error when he allied himself with Ahab. The armies of Judah and Israel were soundly defeated by the Syrians (or Aramaeans, as they were called). Ahab, who went into battle disguised as an ordinary soldier, was fatally wounded; and Jehoshaphat barely escaped with his life.

Ahab was no coward. He ordered his men to prop him up in his chariot, and although he was bleeding to death, he remained facing the enemy all day until the evening, when he died. His body, we are told in the Bible, was brought back to the capital and buried; and one of his servants washed the blood-stained chariot "in the pool of Samaria".

There are descriptions in the Bible not only of Ahab's crimes but of the wealth and importance of Samaria during his reign. The Bible mentions "the ivory house which Ahab built"; and in the present century archaeologists have been able to prove the truth of the Bible description. Teams of British and American archaeologists who were excavating the hill of Samaria found the freshly dug ground full of pieces of yellowish-brown ivory. Most of the fragments were tiny, or blackened by fire; but among them were some larger pieces which could be examined. The archaeologists found that a Hebrew letter had been scratched on the backs of a number of these pieces; and they thought that the letters had served as a guide to the joiner who had put the fragments together. They decided that there had not been a palace made entirely of ivory; this would have been too costly even for the richest of kings. But they found enough of the large pieces to show that they had been used in the panelling and furniture of a splendidly decorated room. On the north side of the courtyard of what had once been a royal palace they discovered a large man-made basin—or hollow; and this, they thought, might well have been the pool of Samaria in which Ahab's chariot had been washed.

CHAPTER VII

THE PROPHETS ELIJAH AND ELISHA; AND THE END OF THE HOUSE OF OMRI

THE "HOUSE OF OMRI" did indeed come to a violent and terrible end. Ahab was succeeded as king of Israel by his son, Ahaziah, who had ruled for little more than a year when he was killed by a fall from a window. At the time he had been preparing to send an army against the Moabites, who paid yearly tribute to Israel but who had revolted after Ahab's death. "Mesha king of Moab was a sheepmaster", says the Bible; "and rendered unto the king of Israel an hundred thousand lambs, and an hundred thousand rams, with the wool. But it came to pass, when Ahab was dead, that the king of Moab rebelled against the king of Israel."

Ahaziah was succeeded by his brother Jehoram (or Joram, as he was also called). Jehoram joined forces with Jehoshaphat, who was still king of Judah, and with the king of Edom, the country to the south-east; and the three kings marched against the rebellious Moabites. The march took them round the southernmost tip of the Dead Sea; and in that dry and desolate country "there was no water for the host, and for the cattle that followed them". The kings were extremely worried; and Jehoshaphat, who was a very religious man, asked Jehoram if he knew of any prophet "that we may enquire of the Lord by him?"

Jehoram, who made an investigation, was told that a much respected prophet called Elisha, a pupil of Elijah, was in the neighbourhood. When Elisha appeared he turned angrily away from Jehoram, a worshipper of idols, but for the sake of the righteous Jehoshaphat he consented to give his advice. The best plan, he said, would be to dig ditches which would bring the much needed water from Edom. "For thus saith the Lord," he declared, "ye shall not see wind, neither shall ye see rain; yet that valley shall be filled with water, that ye may drink, both ye, and your cattle, and your beasts. And this is but a light thing in the sight of the Lord: he will deliver the Moabites also into your hand."

Digging was immediately started. As the ditches were dug water seeped into them; and the water took on the reddish-brown tint of the soil from which it came. When the Moabites saw the water glinting in the early morning sunshine they thought it was blood. "The kings are surely slain, and they have smitten one another," they cried. "Now, therefore, Moab, to the spoil!" The Moabites advanced in a care-free way. They were beaten off by the allied armies, which pursued them, destroying fortresses and laying waste the land as they advanced. King Mesha of Moab, driven back to his last fortress, tried to break through the forces which surrounded him but could not do so. Then, in despair, he killed his own son on the battlements and offered him as a sacrifice to his god, Chemosh. The Israelites, shocked at this outrage, "departed from him and returned to their own land".

For hundreds of years scholars pondered on the reason why the victorious armies had withdrawn without storming the fortress and capturing Mesha. Then, in the nineteenth century, the problem was solved. In 1868 a German missionary, F. A. Klein, was touring Palestine on horseback visiting places mentioned in the Bible. He was passing through ancient Moab (it is now part of the State of Jordan) and came to the remains of the capital, Diban (now called Dibon). There he noticed a large, smooth stone which was almost completely covered in drifting sand. He jumped off his horse to have a closer look at the stone; and when he had

cleared away the sand he saw on one side thirty-four lines of
writing which looked to him like Hebrew. Clearly the stone was
very important; but although the missionary would have liked
to take it away with him it was far too heavy to lift. He was just
beginning to copy the writing when a band of Arabs rushed towards him, shouting that the stone was theirs. They offered to sell
it to him at an enormous price, which he could not possibly afford;
and so he had to depart, after marking the exact site on his map.

Instead of continuing his journey Klein went back to Germany
in order to try and collect the money to buy the stone. Meanwhile, a French scholar in Jerusalem, Charles Clermont-Ganneau,
who had heard about the stone, went at once to Diban to see what
he could do. The Arabs refused to let him remove the stone;
but after a good deal of argument they allowed him to take a
"squeeze"—or impression—of the writing on wet pulp-paper.
When Clermont-Ganneau showed the impression to members of
his government they agreed to buy the stone; but by the time he
returned to Diban with the money the stone had disappeared.
The Arabs had broken it up and removed the pieces, thinking that
they would get a better price if they sold each piece separately. A
great search was started; and in the end most of the pieces were
found. The "squeeze" showed exactly how they had fitted
together; and when the stone had been mended it was taken to the
Louvre Museum in Paris.

The writing on the stone was then translated by scholars. It
proved to be a memorial in the local Moabite language (which
was very like the Hebrew of the Bible) which had been made by
Mesha, king of Moab. "Omri, king of Israel," the memorial
stated, "afflicted Moab many years, because Chemosh was angry
with his land. And his son succeeded him; and he too said, I will
afflict Moab in my days." But later on the god Chemosh, who
had allowed the Israelites to subdue Moab, relented and restored
it to the Moabites. Mesha recaptured his lost cities; "and Israel
perished for ever".

The scholars realised that the Bible had told only one half of the story. The Israelites had "returned to their own land" not simply because they were shocked—as indeed they were—by the dreadful sacrifice of Mesha's son, but because Mesha had broken out of the trap and driven them back.

The writing on the Moabite stone did not mean that Israel had perished for ever; it referred to the fall of the house of Omri. This was brought about by Jehu, an ambitious and utterly ruthless officer in Israel's army. By this time, although Jehoram was still king of Israel, Jehoshaphat's grandson, Ahaziah, was king of Judah. The two kings were allies; for Ahaziah was Jehoram's nephew, the son of his sister, Athaliah; and Athaliah was the daughter of Ahab. The kings of Israel and Judah were at war with Syria. Jehoram was wounded in a battle and returned to Jezreel; and his nephew Ahaziah followed to see if he had been badly hurt. Jehu then seized his chance. He had himself proclaimed king of Israel by his fellow officers. Then he drove furiously to Jezreel, where he murdered the two kings and the aged queen Jezebel. After this slaughter he hunted down and killed all the remaining members of Ahab's family.

According to one Bible story Elijah had been ordered by God to anoint Jehu secretly as king. In another story Jehu was encouraged to revolt by Elijah's pupil, Elisha, because of the idolatry of the king and his family. Jehu worshipped God; but he was violent and cruel in his faith. When he had stamped out the house of Omri he went on to slaughter all the idol worshippers he could find. The writer of this story wanted to make it appear that God had approved of the slaughter and showed this approval by allowing Jehu to reign for twenty-eight years and his son, Joahaz, for seventeen. We do not really know if Elijah or Elisha encouraged Jehu to revolt. But we do know that during the reign of Jehu's great-grandson, Jeroboam II, another great prophet—Hosea—condemned the murders as wicked. Hosea, as we shall see, foretold the end of the kingdom of Israel; and he thought that this would not be too severe a penalty for the slaughter which Jehu had carried out.

Elisha, like Elijah, tried to win people back to the worship of God; and his own faith was as strong as his master's. We are told in the Bible that not long before Elijah died he asked the younger man what he could do for him. "I pray thee," replied Elisha, "let a double portion of thy spirit be upon me." He did not yet feel sure of his own powers; and, when Elijah died, he cried out in despair: "My father, my father, the chariot of Israel, and the horsemen thereof." By this he meant that Israel had lost her greatest strength; for in the chariots and horsemen lay the strength of an army.

Elisha was not as great and heroic a man as Elijah; but he cared very deeply for the people. He lived among them, moving from place to place, rather as Samuel had done before him. Everybody seems to have known and respected him; and when help was needed he was always near at hand, just as he was when Jehoshaphat wanted advice.

Two of the stories told about Elisha show his special care for the people. Once a widow came to him in great distress. Her husband, she said, had been heavily in debt when he died. She could not repay the debt; and the man from whom her husband had borrowed demanded in return that her two sons should become his slaves for life. Debt-slavery, as this unjust custom was called, was quite usual at the time; and in some countries in the East it continued until quite modern times. But Elisha was determined that the woman should not suffer. "What shall I do for thee?" he asked. "Tell me, what hast thou in the house? And she said, Thine handmaid hath not anything in the house, save a pot of oil." Elisha told her to borrow as many empty jars from her neighbours as she could. "And when thou art come in, thou shalt shut the door upon thee and upon thy sons, and shalt pour out into all those vessels, and thou shalt set aside that which is full." From her single jar of oil, we are told, the widow and her sons filled all the borrowed jars. When the last one was full the oil stopped flowing. The woman "told the man of God, And he said, Go, sell the oil, and pay thy debt, and live thou and thy children of the rest."

The second story tells how Elisha helped a young woman who was in no need of money. This woman lived with her husband in a town called Shunem. She had often seen Elisha passing by with his servant, Gehazi, and had invited him into the house to eat. But she wanted to do more for the prophet than this. "Behold now," she said to her husband, "I perceive that this is an holy man of God, which passeth by us continually. Let us make a little chamber, I pray thee, on the wall; and let us set for him there a bed, and a table, and a stool, and a candlestick: and it shall be, when he cometh to us, that he shall turn in thither." Her husband did as she suggested; and Elisha was so grateful that he sent Gehazi to the Shunammite woman to ask what he could do in return. She replied that she needed nothing; but Gehazi, who knew that she had no children, told his master that what she really longed for was a son. Elisha then promised the woman that within a year she would have her wish; and the following spring she gave birth to a son.

The child flourished, and when he was old enough he used to go with his father and the farm workers into the fields. But one day he suddenly cried out, "My head, my head." The father, who saw that his son was very ill, had him carried home to his mother. The boy lay for hours unconscious in his mother's arms, and towards evening he died. His mother carried him up to Elisha's room and laid him on the bed. Then she shut the door, and set out as fast as she could to find Elisha who was, as she knew, on Mount Carmel. Elisha, who saw her coming, sent Gehazi down to meet her, and told him to ask: "Is it well with thee? Is it well with thy husband? Is it well with the child?" And because the woman would only tell the sad news to Elisha himself she answered, "It is well." But Elisha realised that something was wrong. "And when she came to the man of God to the hill, she caught him by the feet: but Gehazi came near to thrust her away. And the man of God said, Let her alone; for her soul is vexed within her." When Elisha learned what had happened he handed Gehazi his staff and told him to go straight to Shunem and place the staff on the child's face. But the mother said to Elisha, "As the Lord liveth, and as thy soul liveth, I will not leave thee. And he arose, and followed her."

When they reached the house Gehazi told them that the child showed no signs of life. Elisha went up to his room, closed the door and prayed to God. "And he went up, and lay upon the child, and put his mouth upon his mouth, and his eyes upon his eyes, and his hands upon his hands: and he stretched himself upon the child; and the flesh of the child waxed warm." After a time the boy sneezed and opened his eyes; and Elisha called the mother and placed the living child in her arms.

The writer of this story was sure that, with God's help, Elisha had worked a miracle. But it is also possible that the boy had not been dead but only deeply unconscious; and that Elisha had revived him by a method which we sometimes hear about today, and which is called "the kiss of life".

Another story told about Elisha shows that the writer's ideas of right and wrong were still very primitive. Elisha was on his way from Jericho to Bethel, and a gang of small boys ran after him, jeering, " 'Go up, thou bald head; Go up, thou bald head.' And he turned back, and looked on them, and cursed them in the name of the Lord. And there came forth two she bears out of the wood, and tare forty and two children of them."

When we read stories such as this, which tell of the killing of people who had done no real harm, it is impossible to believe that God really planned or approved the savage punishments described. What we do know is that the men who wrote these stories down believed that wrongdoing was always punished by God, and that, since in the story of Elisha, the children had jeered at God's prophet, it was only right that they should suffer for it.

The writer of the history of Jehu's revolt, as we saw, made it seem that God approved the slaughter of the house of Omri. The dreadful massacre carried out by Jehu in Israel spread to Judah. After the murder of her son Ahaziah, Athaliah, the queen mother, a cruel and heartless woman, ordered the rest of her own children and grandchildren to be killed in order that she might reign herself. Athaliah ruled for five years—from 841 to 836. She did not know it but one of her grandsons, a little boy named Jehoash, had been hidden by his nurse, and was brought up in secret by the high priest, Jehoiada. When the boy was seven years old Jehoida anointed him king.

During Athaliah's reign idol worship had spread and the Temple at Jerusalem had fallen into decay. Jehoash had the Temple repaired; and he restored the worship of God in Judah with far less violence than Jehu had used in Israel.

Although the writer of the grim tale of Jehu's rise to power made out that God showed his approval by allowing Jehu and his son Jehoahaz to rule Israel for a total of forty-five years, he had very little to say about what happened during those years. We are told that "in those days the Lord began to cut Israel short; and Hazael [by that time king of Syria] smote them them in all the coasts of Israel." Israel, then, was losing ground to Syria; but the writer says nothing about Jehu's far more powerful enemy, Shalmaneser III, king of Assyria.

Shalmaneser's westward advance had been checked, as we saw, by an alliance of kings, among whom "Ahab the Israelite" had the strongest force. Shalmaneser's records were inscribed on a black stone four-sided obelisk—or pillar—which was discovered in 1845 by A. H (later Sir Henry) Layard, a young Englishman who had recently become very interested in archaeology and made some very exciting discoveries. The obelisk was dug up on an ancient mount at Nimrud on the River Tigris, which had once been Shalmaneser's capital. On it the tale of Shalmaneser's triumphs is told in writing and pictures which show the tribute paid to him by his defeated rivals. In one picture the proud and ruthless Jehu of Israel is seen humbly crouching on his hands and knees before the mighty king of Assyria.

Shalmaneser's triumph over Jehu occurred only about twelve years after the battle at Qarqar which had halted Assyria's advance. And so it is clear that, whatever else he did, Jehu did not bring prosperity and strength to Israel, which became a subject state of the Assyrian empire.

In the years which followed Israel was weak and unimportant. It happened that, during the reign of Jehu's great-grandson Jeroboam II who ruled from 783 to 742, there were signs that she might recover. Jeroboam won back large areas of land which had been lost during the reigns of Jehu and his son. But Jeroboam reigned during a period when Assyria was ruled by less warlike kings than Shalmaneser; and after his death Israel became a subject state once more.

In the meantime, one great prophet after another began to deliver his message. And in these messages, which the prophets themselves wrote down, we can see how the idea of right worship and a good way of life really grew.

CHAPTER VIII

THE FIRST OF THE "WRITING" PROPHETS: AMOS AND HOSEA

THE PROPHETS WHO preached from the middle of the eighth century onwards are known as the "writing" prophets because the books which are called by their names were written while they were alive. We do not know if all the prophets could write; but if they could not do so somebody else wrote down their actual words. The prophets were absolutely sure that God had commanded them to speak, and they spoke in His name. They believed that God, who had rescued the Israelites from slavery in Egypt, had given them special duties to worship Him and to serve their fellow men.

During the long reign of Jeroboam II, in which Amos, the first of the "writing" prophets delivered his message, Israel prospered. Jeroboam reigned for forty-one years and, as the Bible reports, "he restored the coast of Israel from the entering of Hamath unto the sea of the plain". This means that once more the kingdom stretched from Syria in the north to the Dead Sea in the south.

Signs of Israel's prosperity came to light during the 1930's. In the storehouse of a palace in the ruins of ancient Samaria archaeologists found large numbers of potsherds—broken pieces of pottery. The potsherds were inscribed with writing which, when translated, proved to be lengthy lists. These lists noted the goods received by Jeroboam or one of his successors, as part of the taxes which he drew from neighbouring districts of Israel. They included corn and wine, and oil which was used by the rich to anoint their bodies. The potsherds were signed by the farmers who had to provide the goods and by the stewards of the king's treasury who took them on his behalf. It is clear from the amounts, which were very large, that the farmers were being very heavily taxed. And because some of the names inscribed on the potsherds end with the syllable "baal" (Meribaal was one of them) the experts realised that once again the baal as well as God was being worshipped in Israel.

Beautiful brown carved ivories which belonged to the same period were also discovered in Samaria. Some of them were decorated with designs in gold, jewels or coloured powdered glass; and they showed that the rich and nobly born were able to surround themselves with lovely, expensive things.

Trade between Israel and foreign countries helped to make Israel prosperous; and Jeroboam was able to build a number of new cities. But this prosperity brought evils with it. Many of the farmers were quite unable to pay their taxes; and the rich seized their chance and bought up the poor farmers' land very cheaply. The loss of their land only served to make the farmers' life harder; and the rich, who had grown proud and unscrupulous, began to oppress them in all sorts of ways. An unscrupulous trader would alter the balance of his scales so that he got his price while his customers received less than their fair share of goods. A judge who was called on to settle a dispute would give his verdict in favour of the man who offered him the highest bribe. Even the priests, who should have set a good example, had grown lazy and ignorant. Outwardly, at any rate, the people were still religious. At festival times they gathered at the sanctuaries to feast and offer sacrifices to God. But the rich continued to oppress their neighbours; and in the whole of Israel there seemed to be no one to take up the cause of the poor.

There was no one in Israel, but there was such a man in Judah. His name was Amos and about the year 760 B.C. he was living in the village of Tekoa, some seven miles to the south-east of Bethlehem. Amos was neither rich nor important. He was a shepherd, who tended a flock of the country's stumpy, thick-fleeced sheep in the Judean hills. He was also a "dresser" of the sycamore trees which grew in this barren district. The sycamore tree produced a crop of hard little fruit something like a fig; and the dresser's job was to scratch the skin of the fruit to make it ripen more quickly.

The Bible does not tell us how Amos learned what was going on in the northern kingdom. He may have gone there once a year to sell the wool from his sheep; or he may have talked to traders from Israel who were travelling to Egypt to buy and sell. We only know that in the silence of the Judean hills he was filled with an urge which he could not resist to leave his home. "The Lord", he said, "took me as I followed the flock, and the Lord said unto me, Go, prophesy unto my people Israel." There was no doubt at all in the mind of Amos that this was God's solemn command. Without hesitating for a moment he set out for Israel; and after walking for about twenty-five miles he reached the sanctuary of Bethel, which at this time was Israel's religious centre.

We can picture the shepherd in his coarse wool cloak as he strode boldly into the court of the temple which, because of its importance, was known as the king's sanctuary. He must have looked very out of place among the richly dressed nobles of Israel. Perhaps they laughed at him; but when he began to speak from the steps of the temple the power of his words silenced them.

"The Lord will roar from Zion, and utter his voice from Jerusalem; and the habitations of the shepherds shall mourn, and the top of Carmel shall wither."

Amos spoke first of the wickedness of the surrounding nations, of Syria, Philistia—the country of the Philistines—of Phoenicia and Moab. These and other nations robbed, plundered and murdered in order to extend their borders; and, he said, as a just punishment, God would bring about their defeat.

Talk of this kind probably pleased his hearers, who would have had no objection to the downfall of their enemies. But, as soon as Amos was sure that he had gained their full attention, he went on to denounce the people of Israel and Judah; and he spoke of the two nations as if they had still been one.

"Hear ye this word which I take up against you, even in lamentation, O house of Israel. . . .

"Ye who turn judgment to wormwood, and leave off righteousness in the earth. . . .

"For as much therefore as your treading is upon the poor, and ye take from him burdens of wheat: ye have built houses of hewn stone, but ye shall not dwell in them; ye have planted pleasant vineyards, but ye shall not drink wine of them.

"For I know your manifold transgressions and your mighty sins: they afflict the just, they take a bribe, and they turn aside the poor in the gate. . . ."

Unless the people repented of their sins and mended their ways they would be punished.

"Seek good, and not evil, that ye may live: and so the Lord, the God of hosts, shall be with you, as ye have spoken.

"Hate the evil, and love the good, and establish judgment in the gate: it may be that the Lord God of hosts will be gracious unto the remnant of Joseph. . . ."

Amos was the first of the prophets who spoke out for social justice. He made it clear that the rich and nobly born had no right to oppress the poor; and that the poor were entitled to justice and fair dealing and to their share of the good things of the earth. Men who denied the poor their rights were not living a good life; and without a good life the feasts and sacrifices they held in God's honour had no meaning. God therefore despised their feast-days. He took no pleasure in their solemn assemblies; and would not accept their offerings of meat and grain:

"Take thou away from me the noise of thy songs; for I will not hear the melody of thy viols.

"But let judgment run down as waters, and righteousness as a mighty stream."

Amos went on to describe the crimes committed against the poor. The rich, he said, made themselves beds of ivory from Samaria. They ate only the most tender meat, the lambs and calves from the flocks and herds. They anointed themselves with costly oil. They drank wine by the bowlful, while the poor went hungry and thirsty. They had cut themselves off from the poor and humble; and for this crime they would be punished. Thus they would be the first of those who would be sent into exile:

"Behold I will raise up against you a nation, O house of Israel, saith the Lord the God of hosts; and they shall afflict you from the entering in of Hemath unto the river of the wilderness."

Although Amos did not speak the name of this nation, no one could have doubted that he meant Assyria. As everybody knew, when the king of Assyria decided to show his power again there would be no resisting him.

The Bible does not tell us how often Amos delivered his message or how long the people went on listening; but we know that some of his words were taken very seriously indeed. He had seen God in a vision, he declared, standing upon a wall made by a plumb-line,* with a plumb-line in his hand.

* i.e. a wall which the builder had measured with a plumb-line to make sure it was straight.

"Then said the Lord, Behold I will set a plumb-line in the midst of my people Israel: I will not again pass by them any more:

"And the high places of Isaac shall be desolate, and the sanctuaries of Israel shall be laid waste; and I will rise against the house of Jeroboam with the sword. . . ."

These words were reported to Amaziah, the high priest. Amaziah, who was perfectly satisfied with conditions as they were, was very much annoyed by the trouble which Amos was trying to stir up. He therefore declared that the prophet was committing treason by threatening the king; and he sent a message to Jeroboam, who was in Samaria thirty-five miles away. "Amos hath conspired against thee in the midst of the house of Israel", the message ran; "the land is not able to bear all his words."

Jeroboam does not seem to have taken any notice of the message; but the high priest did his best to get rid of the troublesome prophet. "O thou seer," he cried, "go, flee thee away into the land of Judah, and there eat bread, and prophesy there; But prophesy not again any more at Beth-el: for it is the king's chapel, and it is the king's court."

Amos replied modestly that he was not a seer—or prophet. He was not even one of the "sons" of the prophets. He was only a simple herdsman and a dresser of sycamore trees; but God had called him to prophesy. And so he refused to obey Amaziah's order and continued to deliver his message.

In the past everybody, from the king and the high priest downwards, had believed that, as God's chosen people, they might expect special benefits and privileges. This was not so, Amos now told them. It was true that God had delivered them from slavery; but that was an act of justice, and He had also delivered others from captivity. In the eyes of God, said Amos, all men were equal whatever their race or colour.

"Are ye not as children of the Ethiopians unto me, O children of Israel? saith the Lord. Have not I brought up Israel out of the land of Egypt? and the Philistines from Caphtor, and the Syrians from Kir?"

Amos believed that the Israelites were God's chosen people. To him, this did not mean that they were entitled to special benefits, but meant instead that they were a people who must accept the privilege of doing God's will. And he told them that the memory of all that their ancestors had suffered as slaves should make them more sympathetic towards those people who were still oppressed.

There was another belief which all the people of the day accepted, Amos among them. This was belief in the "Day of the Lord". The people imagined that on that day they would triumph over all their enemies; but Amos thought of it as a day of judgment, on which Israel would receive equal justice with the other nations.

We do not know what happened to Amos after he had completed his message. It may be that the king or the high priest banished him from Israel. All we know is that his message was written down; and that scholars think that most, if not all, of it was written in his own words. The message was in some ways a harsh one. Amos spoke chiefly of justice. He struggled to make the people believe that every one was entitled to justice; but he did not seem to know, as the prophets who came after him knew, that justice can be softened by mercy.

Some ten or fifteen years after Amos arrived in Bethel a new prophet began to preach. His name was Hosea, and his home was in Israel, unlike Amos and the other writing prophets who all came from Judah.

Hosea's message also predicted that the people of Israel would be punished with captivity for the crimes they had committed, for their injustice and selfishness towards the poor and humble. But Hosea spoke more gently than Amos and with more understanding, perhaps because he was a man who suffered deeply in his own life.

When Hosea began to speak in about 745 B.C., Israel was still a rich and flourishing nation; but the long and prosperous reign of Jehu's descendant, the strong king Jeroboam, was drawing to an end. Jeroboam died in 743; and his death was followed by chaos. Zechariah, Jeroboam's son, who succeeded his father, was murdered by a usurper after a reign of only six months. For the next twenty years one king followed another, and one after another they were deposed or murdered.

Scholars agree that the greater part of the book of Hosea is written in his own words; but in places the language is very difficult to understand. Hosea's own story, which is told in the first three chapters of the book, is a strange and sad one. He married a woman named Gomer; and she was so worthless that the Bible refers to her as "Gomer-not-worth-a-fig". Hosea probably married her because he thought he might be able to persuade her to live a better life; but in this he failed.

Gomer had three children, two sons and a daughter; and Hosea gave them names which showed his own failure to reform his wife, and Israel's failure to reform as a nation. The elder son was called Jezreel, after the battleground where Jehu's murders had been committed. To Hosea, the slaughter was utterly wrong; and it made no difference that it had been committed in the name of religion. He had been ordered by God, he said, to call the child Jezreel; "for yet a little while, and I will avenge the blood of Jezreel upon the house of Jehu, and will cause to cease the kingdom of the house of Israel. And it shall come to pass at that day, that I will break the bow of Israel in the valley of Jezreel."

The second child—a girl—was called Lo-ruhamah, or "Not pitied". This, said Hosea, meant that God would have no more pity on Israel. The name of the youngest child—Lo-ammi—meant much the same; for, translated, it reads, "Not my people".

Hosea used the names of his children and the behaviour of his wife to drive home the meaning of his message. He seems to have loved Gomer dearly, but she ran away from him. Some time later he found her again in the slave market, penniless and about to be sold. He bought her himself, and took her back to his home; but for a while he refused to allow her to leave the house.

Gomer had been a faithless wife; and Hosea compared her with Israel, who was faithless to God. The people would be punished for their crimes; but if they truly sought God there would be forgiveness. They must mend their ways towards their fellow men; and they must change the ceremonial and sacrifices of their worship into real worship: "For I desired mercy, and not sacrifice; and the knowledge of God more than burnt offerings.' Then, said Hosea, God would speak as a loving husband. "I will betroth thee unto me for ever; yea, I will betroth thee unto me in righteousness, and in judgment, and in loving kindness, and in mercies. I will even betroth thee unto me in faithfulness: and thou shalt know the Lord."

CHAPTER IX

ISAIAH, THE PROPHET OF JERUSALEM

DURING THE FIRST half of the eighth century, while Israel prospered under Jeroboam II, Judah also had a strong king. His name was Uzziah and, like Jeroboam's, his reign was a long one. Uzziah strengthened his country's defences, built up trade with foreign nations, and improved farming methods. He was a very religious man, a firm believer in God; and during his reign the people flocked to the Temple to worship and offer sacrifice. In the last few years of his life Uzziah suffered from the dreaded disease of leprosy which was very common in the Middle East; and when he grew too ill to rule his son, Jotham, took over the government in his name and succeeded him as king when he died in 739 B.C. Under Jotham Judah remained rich and prosperous, for Uzziah had done much to help his country. But, as in Israel, the wealthy and the nobly born were becoming idle and luxury-loving, and they, too, were oppressing the humble and the poor.

Round about the time of Amos's arrival in Bethel a small boy was growing up in Jerusalem. His name was Isaiah, and he became one of the greatest—if not the greatest—of all the prophets. Isaiah was probably of noble birth, possibly related to the king; and he was almost certainly a friend of the royal family, free to come and go at court as he pleased.

Isaiah's message is set down in the first thirty-nine chapters of the book of Isaiah. Most scholars agree that the last twenty-seven chapters were not his work but belong to a later age. We shall read about them elsewhere in this book.

By the end of Uzziah's reign Isaiah had grown into a serious, deeply religious young man, who hated and despised the wrong-doing into which his people were slipping.

One day, so the Bible tells us, "in the year that King Uzziah died", Isaiah went, as he must often have gone, to pray in the Temple. As he stood alone before the Holy of Holies he had a vision which utterly overwhelmed him and changed the whole course of his life. "I saw," he said, "the Lord sitting upon a throne, high and lifted up." As he gazed upwards in awe he seemed to hear an angelic voice chanting, "Holy, holy, holy, is the Lord of hosts: the whole earth is full of his glory. And the posts of the door moved at the voice of him that cried, and the house was filled with smoke."

Then Isaiah learned that he must undertake a hard task. He must give up his easy, pleasant life and preach to the people of Jerusalem. At first, like Moses before him, he was overcome by a sense of his own weakness and unworthiness. But, we are told, an angel touched his lips with a live coal which was burning on the altar, and said to him: "Lo, this hath touched thy lips; and thine iniquity is taken away, and thy sin purged. Also I heard the voice of the Lord, saying, Whom shall I send, and who will go for us? Then said I, Here am I; Send me."

The young man was then told that though he must spend his life preaching and prophesying he would not be believed; but even though he knew that this would bring him much unhappi-ness he dared not refuse. The force within him which drove him to his task was stronger than anything else in his life. As another great prophet—Jeremiah—put it, the force was like a burning in his bones.

The message which Isaiah preached was one of doom and disaster for a people who had disobeyed the commands of their religion. He was not a simple shepherd like Amos, but a man who understood very well what was going on in the world. He realised that the kingdoms of Judah and Israel were weak and unimportant compared with empires such as Assyria; and he was able to advise the king not only as a prophet but as a statesman also. He implored the king and the people to put their trust in God; and he saw more plainly than they did the dangers in which they stood. For forty years he spoke to them, trying desperately hard to bring them to a sense of true repentance. But even though he preached disaster, his message was lightened by hope. Judah would perish as a kingdom, he warned them, her people would go into exile; and yet a small number would survive to return to a right way of worship and of life.

The book of Isaiah tells us very little about the prophet's life. We know that he was married; and, since he speaks of his wife as a prophetess, we can be sure that she, at least, took his message to heart. He had two sons and, like Hosea's children, they were given names which had underlying meanings. The elder was called Shear-jashub, which means "the remnant will return". The name of the younger was Maher-shalal-hash-baz, which means "speed, spoil, haste, destruction".

Isaiah's elder son was with him one day when he went to speak to the king. By this time Jotham was dead; but before he died he had done something of which Isaiah had approved. He had been invited to join the kings of Israel and Syria in an alliance against the empire of Assyria, and he had wisely refused. Jotham's son, Ahaz, was a weak and timid king who found it hard to make up his mind. The kings of Israel and Syria had been so much annoyed by his father's refusal to join them that they had launched an attack on Judah. They had already captured a number of fortified cities and were now besieging Jerusalem itself. It seemed to Ahaz that the only thing he could do would be to appeal for help to Assyria.

Isaiah knew what was in the king's mind and was determined to prevent it. He did not think that the king of Assyria would refuse his help; but he was quite sure he would give it only on condition that Judah became one of his subject-states. Ahaz was afraid that his country would be overrun by the armies of Israel and Syria, but Isaiah had no such fear. He compared the two kings with two burned-out firebrands—or torches. They had stirred up strife, but they could do no more harm. "Take heed," he said, "and be quiet; fear not, neither be faint-hearted for the tails of these smoking firebrands." God would deliver Judah, Isaiah assured Ahaz. It would be both wrong and foolish to appeal to the king of Assyria.

Ahaz could not believe the prophet. Isaiah told him to ask God for a sign—any sign he liked—that he was speaking the truth. But Ahaz, who must at last have made up his mind to beg for Assyria's help, refused to ask for any sign at all. Stung by his refusal, Isaiah turned on the king, crying that the Lord himself would give him a sign. A young woman would "conceive and bear a son, and shall call his name Immanuel". The name Immanuel, like the other names, had a special meaning: it meant "God is with us". This child, went on Isaiah, should eat butter and honey so that "he may know to refuse the evil, and choose the good. For before the child shall know to refuse the evil, and choose the good, the land that thou abhorest shall be forsaken of both her kings."

In simple language, Isaiah's prophecy meant that before a child, as yet unborn, was old enough to know the difference between wholesome food and food that is harmful, or the difference between right and wrong (that is to say, while he was still very young) the kings of Israel and Syria would have been defeated. This explanation has always been accepted by Jewish scholars, and it is now also accepted by a number of Christian scholars. But to many Christians—although not to Jews—it has a much deeper meaning. They believe that Isaiah was not speaking about an ordinary child nor about an event which was likely to happen quite soon. They believe that he was prophesying the birth of Jesus of Nazareth, which did not occur for another seven hundred years.

There are other verses in the book of Isaiah which, to Christians, foretell the life and teaching of Jesus. Isaiah spoke of a prince of peace, a perfect king, a wonderful counsellor, who would arise and bring justice, righteousness and peace to the world; and to them this perfect king is Jesus. It is, of course, in the different meanings that Christians and Jews give to passages such as these that one of the chief differences between their religions lies.

Ahaz, king of Judah, could not believe that Isaiah was speaking the truth. He could not bring himself simply to put his trust in God, as the prophet advised. Instead, he sent a message to the king of Assyria, Tiglath-pileser III, imploring his aid against Syria and Israel. Tiglath-pileser, who was an able but ruthless king, willingly agreed to help. He captured Damascus, the capital of Syria; he slew the king; and he took away many captives. Then he turned on Israel. He overran the northern region of the kingdom, and drove out the inhabitants. He set a new king— Hoshea—on the throne, a king who could be trusted to do exactly what he was told; and he forced him to pay tribute to Assyria. He then summoned king Ahaz of Judah to Damascus to pay him homage. Ahaz had got his way; for the tails of the smoking firebrands had been quenched. But the price he had to pay was the price Isaiah had feared. Ahaz himself now had to do what he was told; and Judah became a subject-state of Assyria.

Ahaz does not seem to have worried about this subjection. In order to please his master he adopted many of the customs of Assyria, and worshipped the Assyrian gods. But his country, once so prosperous, quickly grew poor; for Assyria demanded a heavy yearly tribute, which the people were obliged to pay.

Tiglath-pileser died in 727; and after his death Hoshea of Israel decided to rebel against the Assyrian yoke. The new king of Assyria—Shalmaneser V—determined to wipe out this disobedient country. He laid siege to Israel's capital, Samaria. For

Part of an obelisk carved by Shalmaneser III to commemorate his deeds. The scene on the upper panel shows Jehu bowing in front of the king (*courtesy British Museum*)

Part of a series of three slabs showing Sennacherib seated on a throne in front of his tent, receiving spoils from the city of Lachish. From the palace of Sennacherib at Nineveh (*courtesy British Museum*).

three years the city held out; but in 721 B.C. it fell, not to Shalmaneser but to his successor, the usurper, Sargon II. With the fall
of Samaria came the fall of Israel. The kingdom was brought to
an end. The people were dispersed and vanished from history;
and they are remembered only as the lost ten tribes of Israel.

Isaiah lived through these events, but there was nothing he
could do to prevent them. He was devoted to his own country,
and for Jerusalem he had a special love. But he was sure that, as a
nation, Judah was doomed, although he never lost hope that a
remnant of her people would survive. Year after year he preached,
striving to make the people repent of their wrongdoing and live
better lives.

Often he delivered his message in the form of a parable, which
the ordinary people could understand. Once (perhaps it was at
harvest time when the grapes had ripened) he spoke about work
in a vineyard, which all of them knew so well.

"Now will I sing to my wellbeloved a song of my beloved
touching his vineyard. My wellbeloved hath a vineyard in a
very fruitful hill:

"And he fenced it, and gathered out the stones thereof, and
planted it with the choicest vine, and built a tower in the midst
of it, and also made a winepress therein: and he looked that it
should bring forth grapes, and it brought forth wild grapes."

Why should a vineyard which had been so carefully tilled and
planted yield only wild grapes, which were sour and useless? And
what should be done with the barren vineyard? The walls, said
Isaiah, should be broken down, the hedges removed, and the
land left to waste.

"For the vineyard of the Lord of hosts is the house of Israel,
and the men of Judah his pleasant plant: and he looked for
judgment, but behold oppression: for righteousness, but
behold a cry."

There was no doubt about the meaning of this parable. Judah had been lovingly tended by God. Her people had broken His commandments; and for this they would be punished.

All this time the people had been feeling the burden of the Assyrian tribute more and more heavily. Some of the nobles had begun to look elsewhere for help. Their thoughts had turned to Egypt which, until the rise of the Assyrian empire, had been the greatest power in the Middle East, and was still extremely strong. Ahaz was dead by now, and his son, Hezekiah, was king. Hezekiah, who was only twenty when he succeeded his father in about 720 B.C., was a very different kind of man. Ahaz had been weak and timid; Hezekiah was vigorous and clear-headed. Ahaz had worshipped the idols of Assyria; but Hezekiah restored the worship of God.

Even so, Hezekiah was in favour of an alliance with Egypt; and he could not bring himself to believe that Isaiah was right when he begged him—as he had begged Ahaz—to trust in God and not to ally himself with a foreign country. Isaiah spoke of the Egyptian alliance as "a covenant of death"; and, as a sign that, even with Egypt's help, Judah was no match for Assyria, he went about Jerusalem barefoot, clad only in the short cloth worn by prisoners of war.

Sargon, king of Assyria, was killed in 705; and the kings of all his subject-states began to hope that Assyria's hold on them would be loosened. According to the Bible, "In those days was Hezekiah sick unto death." The king who was suffering from a large and very painful abscess, sent for Isaiah, who must have known something about medicine. Isaiah examined him, and then said: "Let them take a lump of figs, and lay it for a plaister upon the boil, and he shall recover." This was done. The hot poultice of figs drew the poison from the abscess and the king quickly recovered. It is interesting to us to know that figs and other fruits and plants which were used in Biblical times as remedies and medicines are still in use today. In some parts of the world, for example, a poultice of chopped up figs boiled in milk is placed on certain kinds of abscess.

After Hezekiah's recovery the Bible tells us that Merodach-Baladan, king of Babylon, sent messengers to congratulate him. Babylonia was one of Assyria's subject-states; but Merodach-Baladan, who had stirred up trouble before, thought that, with the death of Sargon, the time had come for a rebellion. His reason for sending a message of congratulation to Hezekiah was to try and persuade him to join the rebellion.

Hezekiah was delighted to see Merodach-Baladan's messengers. He was flattered by the prince's invitation to join the revolt, and decided to accept. And, as proof of his own importance and of the help he could give, he showed the messengers his weapons of war and the contents of his treasure house.

As soon as the messengers had departed Isaiah came into the king's presence. "What said these men?" he demanded. "And from whence came they unto thee?" Hezekiah explained what had happened. "Then said Isaiah to Hezekiah, Hear the word of the Lord of hosts: Behold, the days come, that all that is in thine house . . . shall be carried to Babylon."

Isaiah's words must have puzzled Hezekiah, for Babylonia was not at this time a powerful empire. The king therefore went ahead with his plans to join in the rebellion and to strengthen the defences of his own country, particularly the fortifications of Jerusalem. In the meantime, Egypt, the only power strong enough to tackle Assyria, had joined the rebels.

If Sargon's successor had been a weak king the rebellion might have succeeded. But the new king, who reigned from 704 to 681, was Sargon's son Sennacherib, a very warlike monarch. Sennacherib's armed forces easily overcame Merodach-Baladon, and went on to inflict a series of crushing defeats on the Egyptian army. They then captured a number of Judah's fortified cities; and, in 701, laid siege to Jerusalem itself.

Their victories were not at all surprising for the Assyrian fighting machine was extremely powerful. It had three arms—

infantry, cavalry, and chariots. The soldiers wore suits of mail, and fought with bows and arrows, slings, swords and spears. But their strongest and most deadly weapon was the battering-ram. This was a heavy beam made of wood and metal, mounted on a siege engine and worked by a crew of three men. The battering-ram was driven with terrific force against the walls of a city; and the mere sight of it was enough to cause panic among the defenders. When a city was forced to surrender there was no mercy for the defeated; nothing but a cruel death or lifelong slavery.

Sennacherib had a boastful account of his many conquests inscribed on a clay cylinder—or prism—copies of which were found among the Assyrian records. He had this to say about the attack on Judah: "As for Hezekiah, the Jew, who did not submit to my yoke, 46 of his strong, walled cities as well as the small cities in their neighbourhood, which were without number. . . . I besieged and took. 200,150 people, great and small, male and female, horses, mules, asses, camels, cattle and sheep without number, I brought away from them and counted as spoil. Himself, like a caged bird, I shut up in Jerusalem, his royal city. . . ."

Reliefs—or wall-carvings—were discovered by Sir Henry Layard in 1845 in Sennacherib's palace at Nineveh, and are now in the British Museum in London. They show the horrors of the siege of Lachish, one of Judah's most important cities. The courageous defenders, very few of them wearing armour, stand on the ramparts hurling down arrows, stones and burning torches. Beneath them the battering-rams are being brought out under the shelter of Assyrian archers; and Assyrian soldiers, armed with helmets and shields and bearing spears and swords, are clambering up the walls. Some of them have already entered the city; for the first captives—men and women—are being led away. As a dreadful example to the defenders, the bodies of the slain are being hung up on stakes for all to see. In the end, the survivors had to give in. And so great was the damage caused by the battering-rams that when, during the 1930's, a British archaeologist, James Lesley Starkey, dug up the remains of the walls, he found in them the huge holes and breaches which these siege-engines had made.

The Lachish wall-carvings also show what happened after the capture of the fortress. In one of them, Sennacherib is seated on a throne before the city, receiving the spoils. The inscription on the carving describes him grandly as, "king of the Universe, king of Assyria".

As one city after another fell to the advancing Assyrians king Hezekiah was preparing Jerusalem for a long siege. In two passages in the Bible—in the Second Book of Kings and in the Second Book of Chronicles—we learn that he deprived the invaders of water and made sure of a plentiful supply in the city. Hezekiah, we are told, "made a pool and a conduit and brought water into the city". And he "stopped the upper watercourse of Gihon and brought it straight down to the west side of the city of David".

King David, as we saw, sent his men through the water-shaft cut by the Jebusites to make a surprise attack on Jerusalem. In those days the only way to get the water was to let down skin buckets into the storage tank below. Hezekiah did not make use of these old workings; and it was quite by chance that, in 1880, his conduit—or channel—was discovered. An Arab schoolboy was bathing one day in the pool of Siloam, a small sheet of water on the hillside above the Kidron Valley. It was known that at one end of the pool there was a narrow entrance to a tunnel into the surrounding rock wall, from which water flowed. Nobody had ever tried to explore the tunnel until the Arab boy squeezed his way through it. Inside, it was very dark; but, as the boy groped his way along, his hand touched an inscribed stone a few yards from the entrance. When he got back he reported his find, and experts were told about it. They examined the rock by the light of torches, and found that the writing was the ancient Hebrew lettering used in the time of Isaiah. The writing reads something like this: "The boring through is completed. And this is the story of the boring: while yet they plied the pick, each toward his fellow, and while yet there were three cubits to be bored through, there was heard the voice of one calling to the other that there was a hole in the rock on the right hand and on the left hand. And on the day of the boring through the workers in the tunnel struck each to meet his fellow, pick upon pick. Then the water poured from the source to the pool twelve hundred cubits, and a hundred cubits was the height of the rock above the heads of the workers in the tunnel."

The inscription on the rock confirms the two passages in the Bible. It also makes it clear that the workmen who had to dig a tunnel through the hard limestone rock had been divided into two gangs, and had started from opposite ends. When, between them, they had hacked their way for about 580 yards one gang could hear the sound of the pick-axes of the other. This must have been a thrilling moment, almost as thrilling as the moment when the two gangs met. The job was a very hard one, for the passage is so narrow that the men had to work in single-file; and although in most parts its height is about six feet, in others it is so low that the men must have done their work crouching. They had no scientific instruments to guide them; and breathing must have been a problem in a tunnel where the air is foul. The experts reckoned that the digging must have taken over six months, and that the workmen had made a marvellous job of it. Working against time, with the Assyrians almost at the gates of Jerusalem, they had made an underground channel which brought the waters of the Gihon spring in the Valley of the Kidron to a safe point within the defence works of the city.

Before the siege started—perhaps while the digging was going on—Sennacherib sent an ambassador to Hezekiah to demand the surrender of the city. Before making any reply Hezekiah sent a message to the prophet Isaiah, asking what he should do; and while he was waiting for Isaiah to answer he went into the Temple to pray earnestly for strength to face the future.

Once again Isaiah counselled complete trust in God. The king of Assyria, he declared, "shall not come into this city, nor shoot an arrow there, nor come before it with shields, nor cast a bank against it. By the way that he came, by the same shall he return, and shall not come into this city, saith the Lord. For I will defend this city to save it for my own sake, and for my servant David's sake."

This time Hezekiah did not hesitate. He took Isaiah's advice. It must have been difficult for him to believe that anything could save the city; but all the same he sent Sennacherib a brave refusal to surrender.

The refusal must have made Sennacherib laugh; and yet, the miraculous happened, and the city was spared. According to the Bible, "the angel of the Lord went out, and smote in the camp of the Assyrians an hundred fourscore and five thousand: and when they arose early in the morning, behold, these were all dead corpses."

What must have happened was an outbreak of one of the death-dealing plagues which were common all over the East. Plague kills swiftly; and the men would have died within a few hours. In the morning the survivors fled in terror from the infection. With them went Sennacherib, never to return. He ruled his empire for another twenty years; and then he was murdered by his own sons as he prayed in the temple of his gods in Nineveh.

We hear no more of Isaiah, after the departure of the Assyrians. By this time he was growing old and his message was completed. Although we do not know what happened to him, he left behind him a book in which there are some of the finest passages in the Bible and some of the greatest thoughts. Year after year he had called on the people to mend their ways: "Cease to do evil, Learn to do well; seek judgment, relieve the oppressed, judge the fatherless, plead for the widow."

He was certain that, as a nation, Judah would cease to exist; but he never wavered in his faith that the righteous few would survive. And he believed that through them, however far away in time it might be, a new and happier age would open, an age in which all people would obey the laws of God. He spoke of this in a passage which is so famous that it occurs again in the Bible— in the book of Micah.

"And it shall come to pass in the last days, that the mountain of the Lord's house shall be established in the top of the mountains, and shall be exalted above the hills; and all nations shall flow unto it.

"And many people shall go and say, Come ye, and let us go up to the mountain of the Lord, to the house of the God of Jacob; and he will teach us of his ways, and we will walk in his paths: for out of Zion shall go forth the law, and the word of the Lord from Jerusalem.

"And he shall judge among the nations, and shall rebuke many people: and they shall beat their swords into plowshares, and their spears into pruninghooks: nation shall not lift up sword against nation, neither shall they learn war any more.

"O house of Jacob, come ye, and let us walk in the light of the Lord."

CHAPTER X

THE PROPHET MICAH; AND THE END OF THE KINGDOM OF JUDAH

HEZEKIAH WAS CERTAINLY one of Judah's best and ablest kings; and, as we saw, he had in Isaiah a wise counsellor and a true friend. Another great prophet preached during his long reign. His name was Micah, and he began to preach about 730 B.C., when Isaiah was a middle-aged man. We do not know if the two prophets ever met; but, as Micah's message is given in words which remind us of Isaiah's, it is likely that the younger prophet was influenced by the older.

Micah came from the village of Moresheth in the Judean hills to the south-west of Jerusalem. It is possible that Moresheth was one of the small cities captured by Sennacherib; but even if it was not destroyed, the Assyrian soldiers may well have stolen the people's crops and farm animals for food.

We know almost nothing about Micah. He was probably a peasant, since he spoke a great deal of the hardships which the country people had to endure; and some scholars have called him "the prophet of the poor" because he was such a champion of their cause. Like the other prophets, he denounced the rich and nobly born for oppressing the poor; and he prophesied that, because of their crimes, Jerusalem would be destroyed.

In the greater part of his book Micah criticises and denounces; but, like Isaiah, he has hope for the future.

"Therefore I will look unto the Lord; I will wait for the God of my salvation: my God will hear me.

"Rejoice not against me, O mine enemy: when I fall, I shall arise; when I sit in darkness, the Lord shall be a light unto me."

One of the most famous passages in the Bible occurs in the book of Micah. In it, the prophet asks a series of questions about how a truly religious person should live, and then he gives the answers. He asks if the worship of God should be accompanied by burnt offerings, the sacrifice of animals, or by the terrible sacrifice of children, a practice which some of the people had copied from their pagan neighbours.

"Wherewith shall I come before the Lord, and bow myself before the high God? shall I come before him with burnt offerings, with calves of a year old?

"Will the Lord be pleased with thousands of rams, or with ten thousands of rivers of oil? shall I give my firstborn for my transgression, the fruit of my body for the sin of my soul?"

The Lord wants none of this, says Micah; and his answer is the truest expression of religion.

"He hath shewed thee, O man, what is good; and what doth the Lord require of thee, but to do justly, and to love mercy, and to walk humbly with thy God."

Hezekiah understood the truth of Micah's message; but not so the kings who followed him. In 692 Hezekiah was succeeded by his son, Manassah. The new king worshipped the idols of Assyria, and even sacrificed his own first-born son to the Assyrian gods. The Bible also tells us that he "filled Jerusalem with innocent blood"; and it is probable that he murdered many of the student prophets who must have tried to prevent the spread of idol worship and its cruel customs.

Manassah's son, Amon, who succeeded him in 638, was no better than his father. Amon was murdered after ruling only a year; but the idol worship which he had encouraged continued during the first years of the reign of Josiah, his son.

Josiah was only eight years old when he became king. As a young boy he was taught by the priests and prophets who were determined to restore the true worship of God; and, as he grew older, he made up his mind to follow the reforms of his great-grandfather, Hezekiah.

During the long reign of Manassah and the short reign of Amon, the Temple had fallen into decay, as it had done earlier in the reign of the murderous queen Athaliah. Josiah, like Jehoash before him, gave orders for the Temple to be repaired. While the work was in progress, the Bible tells us, Shaphan, the Temple scribe, was given some important information by Hilkiah, the high priest. "I have found the book of the law in the house of the Lord," said Hilkiah. Shaphan went at once to the king with the news; and, at Josiah's request, he read the book aloud to him.

Scholars believe that the book was part of the Biblical book of Deuteronomy, which contains one of the two versions of the Ten Commandments and many other laws. In the Bible the book of Deuteronomy is placed last among the five books of Moses, and is written as though the laws were all made by Moses himself. Many scholars think that it was written very much later, during the reign of a king who worshipped idols; but that, out of admiration for Moses, the greatest of the law-givers, it was ascribed to him. They think, too, that the author was a priest or a prophet who was seeking to restore the worship of God. It is also possible that Hilkiah, the high priest, knew all along that the book was in the Temple, and arranged for it to be found at a suitable time.

If this was so, Hilkiah had chosen his moment well; for the young king was deeply moved by the reading. He saw at once that the people had been disobeying many of the laws, and "he rent his clothes" and wept. Everybody must hear the book, he decided; and so "the king sent, and they gathered unto him all the elders of Judah and of Jerusalem. And the king went up into the house of the Lord, and all the men of Judah and all the inhabitants of Jerusalem with him, and the priests, and the prophets, and all the people, both small and great: and he read in their ears all the words of the book of the covenant which was found in the house of the Lord. And the king stood by a pillar, and made a covenant before the Lord, to walk after the Lord, and to keep his commandments and his testimonies and his statutes with all their heart and all their soul, to perform the words of this covenant that were written in this book. And all the people stood to the covenant."

The king then "commanded all the people, saying, Keep the passover unto the Lord your God, as it is written in the book of this covenant." And the Bible adds that "there was not holden such a passover from the days of the judges that judged Israel, nor in all the days of the kings of Israel, nor of the kings of Judah; But in the eighteenth year of king Josiah wherein this passover was holden to the Lord in Jerusalem."

Josiah went on to forbid the worship of idols throughout the country. He closed the sanctuaries where worship had been carried on with pagan practices; and executed the priests who had brought their worship so low. And once again the Temple became the great religious centre of the country. Josiah was a just man and a wise one; and he did his utmost to protect the rights of the poor and to stop their oppression by the rich. The reforms he was making in his own country spread beyond the frontiers of Judah into the country which had once been the kingdom of Israel but was now only a province of Assyria. And Josiah began to dream that one day Israel might be freed from Assyria, and that Israel and Judah would be reunited as they had been in the distant past.

His hopes did not seem impossible; for Assyria was no longer the greatest power in the Middle East. She was threatened by a rival—the empire of Babylonia, in the region of the River Euphrates. But Egypt, still partly under Assyrian rule, was Assyria's ally; and the Egyptian forces, led by Necho, their pharaoh, were marching northwards to Assyria's aid.

Josiah feared that his dream would come to nothing unless he could halt the Egyptian advance and so prevent the Egyptians from joining forces with the Assyrians. With great courage he led his own small army against Necho's. In 609 the two armies met at Megiddo, which guarded the route linking Egypt with the north; but Josiah's army was defeated, and Josiah himself was slain in the fighting.

His death was a disaster for the country. The people at once chose his younger son, Jehoahaz, as the best man to succeed him. But Necho deposed Jehoahaz and made Jehoiakim, his elder brother king instead. Necho knew that Jehoiakim could be trusted to obey his Egyptian masters; and during his reign the great reforms which Josiah had made were all swept away.

The Egyptian mastery lasted only three or four years; for Necho, whose army was again on the march, was soundly defeated by the Babylonian forces. And, with Egypt's downfall, the power of Assyria was broken. Judah was no better off than before. Instead of being a subject state of Assyria or Egypt, she had become the subject of Babylonia.

In 605 an immensely strong man became king of Babylonia. He was Nebuchadnezzar II, and his reign lasted until 562. Jehoiakim of Judah had to pay homage to the new king; and "in his days", the Bible tells us, "Nebuchadnezzar king of Babylon came up, and Jehoiakim became his servant three years."

But when the three years were over Jehoiakim became restless. He listened eagerly to counsellors who advised him to rebel.

When Nebuchadnezzar first heard that Judah was in revolt he did not take the affair very seriously. He left Judah to be crushed by an alliance of some of his other subject states—Moab, Ammon and Syria. When, however, he realised that Judah was holding out, Nebuchadnezzar came himself to take charge of his forces. He was on his way to Jerusalem when Jehoiakim died very suddenly. Jehoiakim's death is a mystery; but it is quite likely that he was murdered. He was succeeded by Jehoiachin, his eighteen-year-old son. Jehoiachin had been king for barely three months when the siege of Jerusalem began. This time there was no out-break of plague to save the city; and the king was forced to sur-render to Nebuchadnezzar. He "went out to the king of Babylon, he, and his mother, and his servants, and his princes, and his officers", the Bible records. With the king and his household went "all the mighty men of valour"—about 7,000 soldiers and 1,000 craftsmen and smiths. We learn that Nebuchadnezzar took prisoner the best and most useful of the people, besides taking as booty the treasure from the Temple. He left a subject king behind in Jerusalem, Mattaniah, Jehoiakim's much younger brother, whose name he changed to Zedekiah.

The capital of the Babylonian empire was Babylon on the Euphrates. Babylon was a city of great magnificence. Its splend-ours were revealed in the years following 1899 by a team of German archaeologists under their leader, Robert Koldewey. Nebuchadnezzar, who had built fortifications for the city and was a warlike king, was also a great planner and builder. He made streets and canals for his city, palaces and temples; and a ziggurat, a high tower, on which stood a temple to the city's god, Marduk. The most famous of all his works were the hanging gardens of Babylon. They were a series of gardens built in terraces, specially planned by Nebuchadnezzar to please his queen. The city also had a wide processional street. It linked the ziggurat with the Ishtar Gate. This Ishtar Gate was a double gate, coloured with bright enamels and flanked by a double wall of fortifications. Babylon was a busy, flourishing city; but it was also strongly guarded, as Jehoiachin must have seen at once.

Although the German expedition made so many important discoveries, it was an apparently dull find which showed that Jehoiachin and the other captives from Judah had been there. Among the discoveries was a collection of inscribed tablets— about 300 of them. They were found in the ruins of a building near the Ishtar Gate and taken to Germany with a number of other finds. Nobody did anything about them until 1933 when an expert made a start on reading and translating them. At first they seemed rather uninteresting; nothing but bills and receipts for goods bought and received. Then, quite suddenly, the translator came upon several lists of oil rations delivered to men who were either prisoners or hostages at the palace. On four of them the same name appeared—"Yaukin, king of the land of Yahud." One of the receipts had the date on it—592. This was five years after the surrender of Jerusalem. The experts knew that "Yahud" was simply another form of the name "Judah"; and, since Jehoiachin would certainly have been a prisoner in Babylon at the time, they realised that "Yaukin" was just a different form of his name.

From the Bible we also learn that Jehoiachin spent many years in prison. Then a new king of Babylonia, Evil-merodach, "in the year that he began to reign did lift up the head of Jehoiachin king of Judah out of prison; And he spake kindly to him, and set his throne above the throne of the kings that were with him in Babylon; And changed his prison garments: and he did eat bread continually before him all the days of his life. And his allowance was a continual allowance given him of the king, a daily rate for every day, all the days of his life."

In the meantime Judah, under Jehoiachin's young uncle Zedekiah, had grown desolate and poor. All the best and most useful of the citizens of Jerusalem were in Babylon; and the people who remained in the other cities were too stricken to try and rebuild their shattered defences or repair their houses. Zedekiah was weak and foolish. For a few years he remained loyal to Nebuchadnezzar, to whom he had taken an oath of allegiance; but then he began to waver. In 588 the pharaoh of Egypt invaded Palestine again; and Zedekiah was persuaded to join him in a revolt against Babylonia.

The revolt was a failure from the start. All it did was to hasten Judah's doom, for when he heard of it, Nebuchadnezzar returned in full force. He set siege to Jerusalem; and while this was going on he wiped out the only two fortified cities which had not been completely destroyed before—Azekah, and Lachish, which had been stormed earlier on by the Assyrians.

The story of the last days of Lachish is a grim one. Part of it is told in discoveries made by the British archaeologist, J. L. Starkey, in 1938. Starkey was examining the ruins of a small room close to the outer gate of the city, which had probably served as a guard-room. In this room, buried in a burnt layer of ashes, he found eighteen inscribed potsherds; and later three more potsherds were found inside the city. The Assyrians had conquered Lachish in 701 B.C.; but these potsherds belonged to the year 588, the year in which Nebuchadnezzar set siege to Jerusalem and stormed Azekah and Lachish. Among the potsherds were a number of despatches sent by a man named Hoshaiah, who was probably an army officer in charge of an outpost, to Joash, a high-ranking officer who was probably in command at Lachish. When the despatches were written Azekah may already have fallen; for in one of them Hoshaiah reports: "We are watching for the signal-stations of Lachish, according to all the signals you are giving, because we cannot see the signals of Azekah."

Lachish seems to have held out at any rate till the autumn of 588, when the olive trees were harvested, for charred olive stones were found among the ashes. Jerusalem held out for eighteen months. When the city surrendered its walls were battered down, the Temple was utterly destroyed, and the houses were burned. Zedekiah, in despair, tried to escape, but was captured and brought back to face a savage punishment. First, he was forced to

look on while his sons were killed; and then his eyes were put out
and he was taken in chains to Babylon. Every man, woman and
child in the country was taken with Zedekiah into captivity, save
for some of the sick and the very poor. Judah, the kingdom of
David whose descendants had ruled for four hundred years, had
come to an end.

CHAPTER XI

JEREMIAH, THE WEEPING PROPHET

WE MUST NOW go over some of the events in the previous chapter again. One of the despatches discovered at Lachish hinted that not all the people of Judah had been behind Zedekiah in his revolt. It refers to some rumours which were being spread at the time, which "are not good, weakening the hands". It seems from the despatch that the men who were advising submission to Babylonia were princes, but a prophet is also mentioned, although not by name. The prophet who counselled peace and submission, and who was accused by the warmongers of "weakening the hands of the soldiers who are left in this city, and the hands of all the people, by speaking such words to them", is thought by some scholars to have been Jeremiah.

Jeremiah preached from about 626 until 586 B.C., the year Jerusalem fell. He was born some time before 642 in a hill village about three miles to the north-east of Jerusalem, and he came from a family of priests. He must have been an extremely sensitive, thoughtful boy; and although he took part in family and village life he never really felt that he belonged. As he grew up his thoughts turned more and more to the wickedness of the world and, in particular, to the sins of the people of Judah. He loved his country, and his whole life was bound up with its fate; and he grieved endlessly because he was certain that disaster would overcome it.

His family had no such fears, and they laughed at him for his misgivings. Throughout his life he was a sorrowful, lonely figure; and he never married and had children of his own. Jeremiah is sometimes called "the man of sorrow" and "the weeping prophet". Some scholars think that he was the author of the book of Lamentations; and the word "jeremiad"—which means lamentation—is derived from his name. Yet, like Isaiah and Micah, Jeremiah held out the hope that a remnant of the people would be saved from the disaster which was coming.

He tells the story of his call to prophesy in the book which bears his name:

"Then the word of the Lord came unto me, saying,

"Before I formed thee in the belly I knew thee; and before thou camest forth out of the womb I sanctified thee, and I ordained thee a prophet unto the nations."

Jeremiah cried out—as Isaiah had cried before him—that the task was too big for him.

"Then said I, Ah, Lord God! behold I cannot speak: for I am a child.

"But the Lord said unto me, Say not, I am a child: for thou shalt go to all that I shall send thee, and whatsoever I command thee thou shalt speak.

"Be not afraid of their faces: For I am with thee to deliver thee, saith the Lord."

The young man knew that people would hate him and his message; yet he dared not refuse the task. He must speak boldly against oppression and injustice, against defiance of Babylonia,

whatever the cost to himself; for the task had been entrusted to
him by God.

"Then I said, I will not make mention of him, nor speak any
more in his name. But his word was in mine heart as a burning
fire shut up in my bones, and I was weary with forbearing, and
I could not stay."

Jeremiah thought first that God had chosen the Scythians, a
cruel and barbarous people from the Caucasus mountains far to
the north, as the instrument of Judah's punishment. The Scythians
were heading south towards Egypt and had overrun the coastal
region of the Mediterranean; and Jeremiah feared that on the way
Judah, too, would be overrun. But suddenly, and without any
warning, the Scythian hordes changed their whole course and
disappeared.

This did not mean that Jeremiah imagined that God had decided
to spare Judah. Babylonia would carry out God's judgment, said
Jeremiah; and he spoke of Jerusalem as a city of desolation and
mourning.

Josiah was king when Jeremiah first began to preach; and the
prophet went about the country urging the people to help the
king in his great work of reform. The priests whose sanctuaries
were being swept away were Jeremiah's enemies. Once, when he
thundered out his message, a priest struck him violently and
condemned him to be put in the stocks all night. During Josiah's
lifetime Jeremiah was not in any real danger; but after the king's
death he was in constant peril. And yet, throughout Jehoiakim's
reign, he preached against the idolatry and the empty worship of
God which had returned when Josiah's reforms came to an end.
The people imagined that they could not be accused of sin if they
went regularly to the Temple to offer sacrifices to God, since the
mere existence of the Temple was their guard. But Jeremiah told
them that empty worship in the Temple itself was no protection
against sin. They could save their country only by reforming

themselves. He spoke to them gravely and earnestly as he stood on the steps of the Temple. "Thus saith the Lord of hosts, the God of Israel, Amend your ways and your doings, and I will cause you to dwell in this place. Trust ye not in lying words, saying The temple of the Lord, The temple of the Lord, The temple of the Lord are these. For if ye throughly amend your ways and your doings; if ye throughly execute judgment between a man and his neighbour; if ye oppress not the stranger, the fatherless, and the widow, and shed not innocent blood in this place, neither walk after other gods to your hurt: then will I cause you to dwell in this place, in the land that I gave to your fathers, for ever and ever." The people, Jeremiah went on, were making no effort to change their ways; and he warned them solemnly, in the name of God, that the Temple would be destroyed as the ancient Temple at Shiloh had been destroyed in the days of the prophet Samuel, and that they would be dispersed and scattered.

Jeremiah's sermon made the priests and the prophets so furious that they seized hold of him roughly, crying, "Thou shalt surely die!" The uproar was heard in the "king's house" nearby, where the princes of Judah were gathered. The priests and prophets were accusing Jeremiah of treason; and so the princes assembled to hear the charge and give judgment. "This man is worthy to die;" cried his accusers, "for he hath prophesied against this city."

Jeremiah faced his judges calmly. He made no attempt to deny what he had said. His only care was that every one should hear his message. "Then spake Jeremiah unto all the princes and to all the people, saying, The Lord sent me to prophesy against this house and against this city all the words that ye have heard. Therefore now amend your ways and your doings, and obey the voice of the Lord your God; and the Lord will repent him of the evil that he hath pronounced against you." He did not ask for mercy from his judges. "As for me," he said, "behold, I am in your hand: Do with me as seemeth good and meet unto you. But know ye for certain, that if ye put me to death, ye shall surely bring

innocent blood upon yourselves, and upon this city, and upon
the inhabitants thereof: for of a truth the Lord hath sent me unto
you to speak all these words in your ears."

The princes, who had listened quietly to the accusation and to
Jeremiah's defence, then considered their verdict. The prophet,
they decided, was innocent. He did not deserve the sentence of
death, "for he hath spoken to us in the name of the Lord our
God." They had not all been in favour of the verdict; and it was
recalled that Uriah—a lesser prophet who had been following
Jeremiah's example—had been put to death on the orders of king
Jehoiakim. But Jeremiah's life was saved because Ahikam, the
most important of the princes, had been on his side, and because
the princes remembered that although Micah had prophesied the
destruction of Jerusalem, king Hezekiah had not ordered his
execution.

So Jeremiah went on preaching his sermons fearlessly. He
attacked the king himself for his idolatry and for using forced
labour to build a magnificent new palace. He opposed Jehoiakim's
plan for an alliance with Egypt, and went on urging submission to
Babylonia. Jehoiakim never forgave him. He did not have him
put to death but took his revenge in another way. When Jeremiah
had been preaching for more than twenty years he was suddenly
forbidden by the king to speak in public places.

The prophet therefore decided to write down his message, and
he dictated it to his friend Baruch, a scribe. Baruch wrote the
whole of the message on a scroll; and then, at the risk of his own
life, he read it aloud to the people who had assembled at the
Temple on a fast day.

The princes of Judah who were still on Jeremiah's side offered
to take the scroll to the king; but they advised Jeremiah and
Baruch to go into hiding. They found Jehoiakim sitting near a
brazier of burning coals in his winter-house, a palace which had
been built to catch the wintry sunshine. Jehoiakim ordered
Jehudi, a scribe, to read the scroll aloud; and as he listened to the
message his anger grew. And so, "when Jehudi had read three or

four leaves, he [the king] cut it with the penknife, and cast it into the fire that was on the hearth, until all the roll was consumed in the fire that was on the hearth." Three of the princes had urged the king not to burn the scroll, but he refused to listen to them. When the whole scroll was burnt to ashes he sent out an order for the arrest of Jeremiah and Baruch; but they had taken the princes' advice and escaped.

Jeremiah was not deterred by the king's action. He dictated a second message to the faithful Baruch. It contained everything he had said in the first, with some additions; and it forms the outline of the book of Jeremiah as we know it in the Bible.

In the book of Jeremiah we get a clear picture of the prophet; for, try as he might, he could not prevent his own feelings from breaking into his message. He was driven by a power, far stronger than himself, to deliver a message of stern rebuke and a prophecy of doom. Yet often he was weak and afraid; and always, except when he felt himself to be in God's presence, he was lonely and unhappy. But just because we know that he was frightened and often complained most bitterly about his fate he seems to us a far more human figure than the other great prophets. Everything he did seemed to go wrong. He had implored Jehoiakim to submit patiently to Babylonia; but the king had listened to the warmongers who counselled revolt; and the revolt had led to the exile of all the finest of the people of Judah.

Jehoiakim himself was now dead; his son, Jehoiachin, was a prisoner; and the weak Zedekiah, who had sworn allegiance to Nebuchadnezzar, was king of Judah. Jeremiah's warnings had come true; but his advice was still unheeded, for there were warmongers in Jerusalem who were trying to rouse Zedekiah to renounce his allegiance. In a desperate effort to show what would happen if Zedekiah rebelled, Jeremiah walked about the streets of the city, wearing twisted wooden bars in the form of a yoke about his neck. This was a sign to the king and the people that if they rebelled they would become the slaves of the Babylonians.

Among the warmongers were prophets who were doing their

best to convince Zedekiah that if he rebelled he would win, and the captives would be released. One of these prophets, a man named Hananiah, confronted Jeremiah one day in the Temple court. In the presence of the priests and the people Hananiah swore that within two years Jehoiachin and the other captives would be freed and the precious objects taken from the Temple would be restored. Jeremiah, who would have liked to believe in the truth of this prediction, called out, "Amen: the Lord do so!" But he went on to remind Hananiah that the great prophets of old had all predicted disaster for Judah. Then in a fit of rage Hananiah tore the yoke from Jeremiah's neck and broke it in pieces. In this way, he boasted, would the Lord break the yoke of Nebuchadnezzar.

Jeremiah went away unconvinced. We next hear of him walking about the streets of Jerusalem saying that Hananiah had broken a yoke of wood, but that the wooden yoke would be replaced by one of iron.

Zedekiah swayed first to one side, then to the other. Sometimes he would listen to Jeremiah, whom he always respected; sometimes to the prophets who urged him to join with Egypt and rebel against Babylonia. Naturally the warmongers hated and feared Jeremiah's influence. They went to Zedekiah and accused the prophet of treason. And Zedekiah gave them permission to arrest Jeremiah and fling him into a water cistern. The cistern was empty, but the bottom was covered in thick, evil-smelling mud. Jeremiah sank into the mire; and he would have died a horrible death but for the kindness of an Ethiopian servant of Zedekiah's called Ebed-Melech. When he heard what had happened Ebed-Melech hurried to the king and begged him to release Jeremiah.

Zedekiah, swayed as ever by the last speaker, gave orders for Jeremiah's release from the cistern. "Take from hence thirty men with thee," he told his servant, "and take up Jeremiah the prophet out of the dungeon, before he die."

Ebed-Melech chose three men. They collected some worn-out clothing and rags; and these they let down with ropes into the cistern. "Put now these old cast clouts and rotten rags under thine armholes under the cords", the Ethiopian told Jeremiah; for he knew that without padding the ropes would cut Jeremiah severely. The prophet did as he was told and was drawn up to safety. He was still officially under arrest, and he was lodged in the guard-house of the prison.

By this time Zedekiah was in a panic. He had given in to the warmongers and rebelled against Nebuchadnezzar; and now the Babylonian army was marching on Jerusalem. In his terror he sent secretly for Jeremiah and begged him for advice. There was only one way to avert the fate of the city, said Jeremiah. Zedekiah must give himself up as a hostage to Nebuchadnezzar. "If thou wilt assuredly go forth unto the king of Babylon's princes, then thy soul shall live, and this city shall not be burned with fire; and thou shalt live, and thine house." Zedekiah could not bring himself to take this advice. He sent the prophet back to prison; and there he remained during the dreadful months of the siege of Jerusalem.

And yet, Jeremiah chose this time of all others to proclaim his faith in the future. One of his uncles had recently died, and a field which belonged to the family was being sold. Jeremiah bought the field from the dead man's son, to show that, even in the midst of disaster, all was not lost. In the presence of witnesses he charged the faithful Baruch to put the signed and sealed deeds of purchase safely in an earthenware vessel, "that they may continue many days. For thus saith the Lord of hosts, the God of Israel; Houses and fields and vineyards shall be possessed again in this land."

Jeremiah remained behind when, after the siege was over, the blinded Zedekiah was dragged with the other captives to Babylon. Jerusalem was in ruins; the Temple was utterly destroyed; and, as we saw, only a few of the poorest of the people were left. But Nebuchadnezzar had appointed a good and able governor of Jerusalem, a Judean named Gedaliah; and Jeremiah knew that he and Gedaliah could work together.

His hopes for the future were now fixed on the exiles in Babylonia; and he sent them a comforting letter of advice. In it, he
urged them in the name of their God to settle down and make the
best of their lives. "Build ye houses, and dwell in them; and plant
gardens, and eat the fruit of them. Take ye wives, and beget sons
and daughters; and take wives for your sons, and give your
daughters to husbands, that they may bear sons and daughters;
that ye may be increased there, and not diminished. And seek the
peace of the city whither I have caused you to be carried away
captives, and pray unto the Lord for it: for in the peace thereof
shall ye have peace." Jeremiah was sure that the children or
grandchildren of the exiles would be chosen by God to return to
Jerusalem and rebuild the Temple; and, meanwhile, they should
behave as loyal citizens of Babylon. "For thus saith the Lord,
that after seventy years be accomplished at Babylon I will visit
you, and perform my good word toward you, in causing you to
return to this place."

The present was dark, but the future, with God's help, would
be bright:

"Therefore fear thou not, O my servant Jacob, saith the Lord;
neither be dismayed, O Israel; for, lo, I will save thee from
afar, and thy seed from the land of their captivity; and Jacob
shall return, and shall be in rest, and be quiet, and none shall
make him afraid."

Although Jeremiah kept his thoughts on the future his own life
ended in sorrow. Gedaliah, the good governor of Jerusalem, was
murdered; and the citizens, terrified that Nebuchadnezzar would
take vengeance on them, decided to flee into Egypt. All through
his preaching life Jeremiah had warned the people against friendship with Egypt. Now he told them solemnly that if they went
they would never return. Scornfully, they accused him of lying.
Then they seized hold of Jeremiah and the faithful Baruch, and
hustled them along in their headlong flight from Jerusalem.

And so Jeremiah, by this time an old man, ended his days in exile in Egypt. Despite his unhappiness he remained sure that one day Jerusalem would rise again. God, he declared, would make a new covenant—or bond—with his people. "Behold, the days come, saith the Lord, that I will make a new covenant with the house of Israel, and with the house of Judah: not according to the covenant that I made with their fathers in the day that I took them by the hand to bring them out of the land of Egypt; which my covenant they brake, although I was an husband unto them, saith the Lord: But this shall be the covenant that I will make with the house of Israel; After those days, saith the Lord, I will put my law in their inward parts, and write it in their hearts; and will be their God, and they shall be my people. And they shall teach no more every man his neighbour, and every man his brother, saying, Know the Lord: for they shall all know me, from the least of them unto the greatest of them, saith the Lord: for I will forgive their iniquity, and I will remember their sin no more."

CHAPTER XII

EZEKIEL, AND OTHER PROPHETS OF THE EXILE

THE JEWS IN Babylonia took Jeremiah's advice and settled down quietly. Life was not harsh or cruel, for Nebuchadnezzar treated them well. He needed their help in his empire-building schemes; and he was wise enough to see that the best way to gain their loyalty was to give them freedom to settle in a fertile part of the country, and to live their lives and worship God as they chose. Many of the exiles became farmers; some went into trade and commerce. But although the older people remained faithful to their God and their own way of life, the children soon learned Babylonian customs; and, as they grew older they began to neglect their religion and the traditions of their parents. They might have been more faithful to their religion if there had been a temple in which they could worship. Nebuchadnezzar was willing for the Jews to build a temple; but their laws forbade it. The only religious centre allowed them was the now ruined Temple in far-off Jerusalem.

The older men and women among the exiles longed hopelessly to return to their own country. One of them wrote a poem (we know it as Psalm 137) which expressed their sadness and longing:

"By the rivers of Babylon, there we sat down, yea, we wept, when we remembered Zion.

"We hanged our harps upon the willows in the midst thereof.

"For there they that carried us away captive required of us a song; and they that wasted us required of us mirth, saying, Sing us one of the songs of Zion.

"How shall we sing the Lord's song in a strange land?

"If I forget thee, O Jerusalem, let my right hand forget her cunning.

"If I do not remember thee, let my tongue cleave to the roof of my mouth; if I prefer not Jerusalem above my chief joy."

These people were badly in need of encouragement and guidance in their homesickness and grief. A number of prophets and poets tried to comfort them; but only one is known to us by name. He is the prophet Ezekiel. We know nothing about Ezekiel except what is written in his book. Scholars think that the greater part of the book was written by Ezekiel in his old age; but some passages in it are confusing, and they think that these were added by later writers.

Ezekiel, like Jeremiah, came from a family of priests. He claimed descent from Zadok, the priest of David's reign; and, through Zadok, he believed he was descended from Aaron, the brother of Moses and the founder of the priests of Israel. Ezekiel grew up in Jerusalem during the lifetime of Jeremiah; but he does not mention the older prophet, and we do not know if he ever met him or heard him speak.

In 597, when Ezekiel was a young man, he was taken to Babylon with Jehoiachin and the first batch of exiles. The Bible tells us that he settled in a village on the "river Chebar", a wide canal which watered an arc of land inland from the Euphrates. Ezekiel seems to have been well treated. He married a wife whom he loved very dearly; and he lived in a house built of sun-dried bricks which was large enough to hold meetings of his fellow exiles.

He had started preaching before he left Jerusalem; and in the first chapter of his book he describes the vision in which he learned that he was to be a prophet. A fearful storm was raging at the time; and, in a storm-cloud pierced by flashes of lightning, he seemed to see strange winged figures which had animal as well as human faces. The air between these creatures was studded with shifting lights; and when the creatures moved, he seemed to hear "the noise of their wings, like the noise of great waters, as the voice of the Almighty. . . . And there was a voice from the firmament that was over their heads." At the sound of this voice Ezekiel fell on his face in awe. But the voice said to him: "Son of man, stand upon thy feet, and I will speak unto thee."

Ezekiel's message to the people of Jerusalem, like the message of the older prophets, was one of rebuke; and he, too, declared that Judah would fall as a punishment for the people's sins. But now the worst had happened; and, in Babylon, Ezekiel's task was not only to rebuke the exiles but also to give them hope. For twenty-two years—from 592 to 570 B.C., he was the guide and counsellor of the perplexed and grieving Jews. His book is written in vivid, poetic language, which is sometimes wild and confusing; and his visions are full of strange, fantastic images. Yet his message shows a big step forward in religious thinking.

Ezekiel urged on the exiles two important ideas. The first was the need for true repentance, which also means amendment. God, declared Ezekiel, had no wish to punish people who were truly repentant: "Cast away from you all your transgressions, whereby ye have transgressed; and make you a new heart and a new spirit: for why will ye die, O house of Israel? For I have no pleasure in the death of him that dieth, saith the Lord God: wherefore turn yourselves, and live ye."

The second idea was entirely new. It was that man is free, and is reponsible for what he does. There was a much-quoted proverb at the time: "The fathers have eaten sour grapes, and the children's teeth are set on edge." The proverb meant that if one generation sinned the next generation would be made to suffer for its wrongdoing. This idea was false, said Ezekiel. "The word of the Lord came unto me again, saying, What mean ye, that ye use this proverb concerning the land of Israel . . .? As I live, saith the Lord God, ye shall not have occasion any more to use this proverb in Israel. Behold, all souls are mine; as the soul of the father, so also the soul of the son is mine: the soul that sinneth, it shall die. But if a man be just, and do that which is lawful and right, . . . he shall surely live, saith the Lord God."

All through the years of his preaching Ezekiel tried to keep the people's thoughts on the future. Their exile would not last for ever, he assured them. As God's people, they would, in a sense, be reborn and renewed; and they would return to Jerusalem and rebuild the Temple.

The prophet described this rebirth of the nation in one of his strangest visions. In it, he seemed to feel the hand of God guiding him into a wide valley in which the bones of men lay bleaching. God asked him if the dead bones could live; and Ezekiel answered: "O Lord God, thou knowest." Then God commanded him to speak to the dry bones, saying: "Behold, I will cause breath to enter into you, and ye shall live: And I will lay sinews upon you, and will bring up flesh upon you, and cover you with skin, and put breath in you, and ye shall live; and ye shall know that I am the Lord." Ezekiel did as he was ordered; and, in his vision, he seemed to see the bones transformed into living men, who "stood up upon their feet, an exceeding great army".

This vision meant that God would revive the dry, dead spirit of His people; and give them the hope and will to rebuild their faith. "Thus says the Lord God: Behold, O my people, I will open your graves, and cause you to come up out of your graves, and bring you into the land of Israel." In the new and better age which would begin, the kingdoms of Israel and Judah would be reunited again; and once more they would be ruled by a member of the family of David. But the return to Jerusalem must be accompanied by a return to true religion. "And I will give them

one heart, and I will put a new spirit within you; and I will take
the stony heart out of their flesh and I will give them an heart of
flesh: That they may walk in my statutes, and keep mine ordin-
ances, and do them: and they shall be my people, and I will be
their God."

Between this splendid vision of Ezekiel's and his final visions
there is a gap of twelve years. We know nothing of what happened to him during that time; but perhaps he was very ill. In
573 B.C. he began to preach again. In his last visions he saw the
rebuilt Jerusalem; and he described to the people exactly how the
new Temple should be planned, with its worship and ceremonial.
He spoke, too, of their faith as a river which issued from the
Temple as a tiny stream; but which grew wider and stronger
until it had changed the wasteland through which it flowed into a
fertile region, teeming with life.

Ezekiel, as we saw, is the only prophet of the exile whose
name is familiar to us. But there are a number of other books in
the Bible called after the prophets who wrote them. These
prophets were all Judeans, for the kingdom of Israel had vanished
in 721 B.C. We know very little about their lives; and some of
their books are only fragments.

One of these prophets was Zephaniah, who lived in Jerusalem
at about the same time as Jeremiah. Zephaniah, who was a great-
great-grandson of king Hezekiah, was the only prophet who
belonged to the royal family of Judah. But this did not make him
proud. Like the other prophets, he denounced the rich and the
nobly born for oppressing the poor and humble; he denounced
the judges who took bribes; the lazy, ignorant priests; and the
people who lapsed into idolatry or empty worship. He predicted
disaster for the kingdom; but he, too, believed that a faithful
remnant of the people would return.

Another prophet who lived about the same time was Nahum.
We know absolutely nothing about Nahum's life; but he
preached against the sins of the Assyrians and predicted the defeat
of their armies. Scholars who have studied his writings think that

The Siloam Tunnel (*courtesy Palestine Archaeological Museum*)

Inscription from the Siloam Tunnel (*courtesy Palestine Archaeological Museum*)

he must have preached shortly before Assyria's capital, Nineveh, was captured by the Babylonians in 612 B.C.

Habbakuk, like Zephaniah, was preaching during Jeremiah's lifetime; but we are not told in the Bible whether they knew one another. Habbakuk delivered his messages between the years 608 and 597; and, like Jeremiah, he was well aware of the strength and importance of Babylonia. When he saw drought and famine, and the cruelty and injustice which went on all around him he wondered how God could allow such evils to exist. But his faith was so strong that he never for a moment doubted God's wisdom:

"Although the fig tree shall not blossom, neither shall fruit be in the vines; the labour of the olive shall fail, and the fields shall yield no meat; the flock shall be cut off from the fold, and there shall be no herd in the stalls:

"Yet I will rejoice in the Lord, I will joy in the God of my salvation."

One of the prophets who spoke words of comfort to the Jews in their exile in Babylonia is famous, although we do not know his name or anything about him. He is the author (or authors) of chapters 40 to 55 of the book of Isaiah; for scholars are not sure if these chapters were all written by the same man. They have called this unknown writer Deutero-Isaiah—or the Second Isaiah; and they believe that his message dates from about the year 540 B.C.

The Second Isaiah's message was one of hope. He summoned the people to faith; and he promised them that Israel would be restored to Jerusalem. The exile had lasted for nearly fifty years when he began to speak; and he believed that the time of punishment was over:

"Comfort ye, comfort ye my people, saith your God.
"Speak ye comfortably to Jerusalem, and cry unto her, that

her warfare is accomplished, that her iniquity is pardoned: for she hath received of the Lord's hand double for all her sins."

The prophet's mind was filled with a splendid vision of the future, and he seemed to hear:

"The voice of him that crieth in the wilderness, Prepare ye the way of the Lord, make straight in the desert a highway for our God.

"Every valley shall be exalted, and every mountain and hill shall be made low: and the crooked shall be made straight, and the rough places plain:

"And the glory of the Lord shall be revealed, and all flesh shall see it together: for the mouth of the Lord hath spoken it."

Man was as nothing compared with God; yet God was loving and merciful towards man:

"The voice said, Cry. And he said, What shall I cry? All flesh is grass, and all the goodliness thereof is as the flower of the field:

"The grass withereth, the flower fadeth: because the spirit of the Lord bloweth upon it: surely the people is grass.

"The grass withereth, the flower fadeth: but the word of our God shall stand for ever.

"O Zion, that bringest good tidings, get thee up into the high mountains; O Jerusalem, that bringest good tidings, lift up thy voice with strength; lift it up, be not afraid; say unto the cities of Judah, Behold your God!

"Behold, the Lord God will come with strong hand, and his arm shall rule for him: behold, his reward is with him, and his work before him.

"He shall feed his flock like a shepherd: he shall gather the lambs with his arm, and carry them in his bosom, and shall gently lead those that are with young."

The Second Isaiah's words must have brought comfort and renewed hope to the weary exiles; and, although they did not know it, the date of their release was not far off. By this time—539 B.C.—Nebuchadnezzar had been dead for just over twenty years. The reigning king was Nabunaid, a usurper and the last of the Babylonian kings. Nabunaid shared the kingship with his son, Belshazzar. The name of Belshazzar appears in the book of Daniel; but, as we shall see, most scholars think that the book of Daniel was written nearly four hundred years later. They think, too, that it was not meant to be read as history, but was written to comfort and encourage the Jews at a time when they were being bitterly persecuted.

The book of Daniel describes a feast which Belshazzar held for himself and his nobles. While they were eating and drinking some mysterious writing appeared on the wall, which nobody could read. Belshazzar, so the story goes, sent for his wise men, but they could not read the writing. Then the queen remembered a man called Daniel, one of the exiles from Judah, who was respected for his wisdom. Daniel was sent for, and he read and translated the writing to the king. The king went cold with fear as he listened to this message: "God hath numbered thy kingdom, and finished it.... Thou art weighed in the balances, and art found wanting.... Thy kingdom is divided, and given to the Medes and Persians."

We may not believe that the story in Daniel is history; but what happened next is certainly true. An army was approaching the city of Babylon. It was led by a man who is known in history as Cyrus the Great. Cyrus was king of Persia. He was a great empire builder; and in 539 B.C. he overcame the Babylonian forces and entered Babylon in triumph.

Cyrus was different from most conquerors, for he was a man of humanity and understanding. His army left no trail of desolation behind it; cities were not destroyed; prisoners were not executed. Cyrus, of course, was a pagan; and the writing on a famous document—the clay Cylinder of Cyrus—describes him as a favourite of the Babylonian god, Marduk: "Marduk ... sought a righteous prince, after his own heart, whom he took by the hand. Cyrus ... he called by name, to lordship over the whole world he appointed him. . . . To his city Babylon he caused him to go, he made him take the road to Babylon, going as a friend and companion at his side. His numerous troops, in number unknown, like the water of a river marched armed at his side. Without battle and conflict he permitted him to enter Babylon. He spared his city Babylon a calamity."

The writing on the cylinder goes on to relate how Cyrus entered Babylon in peace, and how his troops wandered peacefully about the countryside; and it quotes Cyrus as saying: "I let no man be afraid. I concerned myself with the internal affairs of Babylon and all its cities. The dwellers in Babylon . . . I freed from the yoke that ill became them. I repaired their houses, I healed their afflictions. . . ."

Cyrus behaved in a truly fine manner. There were captives from other conquered countries as well as from Judah living in Babylonia; and he gave orders that they should all be allowed to return to their homes. When the Second Isaiah first heard of Cyrus's conquests he foretold that this just and merciful king would end the exile of the Judeans.

"Thus saith the Lord to his anointed, to Cyrus, whose right hand I have holden, to subdue nations before him; and I will loose the loins of kings, to open before him the two leaved gates; and the gates shall not be shut;

"I will go before thee, and make the crooked places straight: I will break in pieces the gates of brass, and cut in sunder the bars of iron:

"And I will give thee the treasures of darkness, and hidden riches of secret places, that thou mayest know that I, the Lord, which call thee by thy name, am the God of Israel.

"For Jacob my servant's sake, and Israel mine elect, I have even called thee by thy name: I have surnamed thee, though thou hast not known me.

"I am the Lord, and there is none else, there is no God beside me. . . ."

Elsewhere, the Second Isaiah wrote of Cyrus as specially chosen by God to restore Jerusalem to its old grandeur:

"Thus saith the Lord, thy redeemer, . . . That saith of Cyrus, He is my shepherd, and shall perform all my pleasure: even saying to Jerusalem, Thou shalt be built; and to the temple, Thy foundation shall be laid."

We learn from the second book of Chronicles that Cyrus made a proclamation throughout the kingdom: "Thus saith Cyrus king of Persia, All the kingdoms of the earth hath the Lord God of heaven given me; and he hath charged me to build him an house in Jerusalem, which is in Judah. Who is there among you of all his people? The Lord his God be with him, and let him go up."

Because the exile of the Jews had lasted so long—nearly fifty years—some of the younger ones had no wish to leave Babylonia, and so they remained there. But to the rest, the thought that they were free to return to Jerusalem and rebuild the ruined Temple was the fulfilment of all their dreams. Joyfully they began to make ready to leave; and we can guess—although the Bible does not tell us—that the Second Isaiah was among them.

If we do not know anything about the life of this prophet, we have his writings, with all their beauty and poetry. But the Second Isaiah has left the world a problem; for the most famous part of his message means one thing to Jews and something entirely different to Christians. In five chapters of the book of Isaiah—chapters 42, 49, 50, 52 and 53—there are passages which are known together as the "Servant" poems. They all refer to a servant, especially chosen by God to serve Him:

> "Behold my servant, whom I uphold; mine elect, in whom my soul delighteth; I have put my spirit upon him: he shall bring forth judgment to the Gentiles.
> "He shall not cry, nor lift up, nor cause his voice to be heard in the street.
> "A bruised reed shall he not break, and the smoking flax shall he not quench: he shall bring forth judgment unto truth.
> "He shall not fail nor be discouraged, till he have set judgment in the earth: and the isles shall wait for his law."

We can tell from this passage that the work of the Servant was to spread from Israel to the whole world. It was not enough for the Servant to serve Israel alone; and God had said:

> "It is a light thing that thou shouldest be my servant to raise up the tribes of Jacob, and to restore the preserved of Israel: I will also give thee for a light to the Gentiles, that thou mayest be my salvation unto the end of the earth."

The task ordained for the Servant was the establishment of justice, peace and love throughout the world; and God would show His Servant how the task should be fulfilled. It would be a hard task and a bitter one; for the Servant would have to fight against ignorance and hatred, poverty and distress. God would give His Servant power and make his mouth "like a sharp sword"; yet the Servant must go about his work humbly and without pride:

> "The Lord God hath given me the tongue of the learned, that I should know how to speak a word in season to him that is weary: he wakeneth morning by morning, he wakeneth mine ear to hear as the learned.

"The Lord God hath opened mine ear, and I was not rebellious, neither turned away back.

"I gave my back to the smiters, and my cheeks to them that plucked off the hair: I hid not my face from shame and spitting.

"For the Lord God will help me; therefore shall I not be confounded: therefore have I set my face like a flint, and I know that I shall not be ashamed."

The Servant would meet with many rebuffs; he would be "despised and rejected of men; a man of sorrows, and acquainted with grief". He would have to suffer from the sins and cruelties of the world:

"Surely he hath borne our griefs, and carried our sorrows: yet we did esteem him stricken, smitten of God, and afflicted."

And yet, even though he would suffer persecution and death, the final victory would be his, for despite his sufferings he would remain faithful to God:

"Yet it pleased the Lord to bruise him; he hath put him to grief: when thou shalt make his soul an offering for sin, he shall see his seed, he shall prolong his days, and the pleasure of the Lord shall prosper in his hand.

"He shall see of the travail of his soul, and be satisfied . . . because he hath poured out his soul unto death: and he was numbered with the transgressors; and he bare the sin of many, and made intercession for the transgressors."

To Christians, these Servant passages came true in the life of Jesus of Nazareth. To Jews, they refer to the people of Israel as God's servant, a servant whose duty is to be "a light to the nations", that God's "salvation may reach to the end of the earth".

The Christian faith has its roots in Judaism—the religion of the Jews. Another of the world's great religions—Islam, the religion of the Muslims—also sprang from Judaism. The people of these three religions all believe in the One God, although they differ in other beliefs. In the past these differences have led to much suffering. But today we realise that we must respect other people's differences, since the great belief we share—faith in the One God —unites us all.

CHAPTER XIII

THE RETURN TO JERUSALEM

IN THE SPRING of 537 B.C. the Jews set out on their eight hundred mile journey from Babylon to Jerusalem. They had with them their servants and their pack-animals; and also the treasures taken from the Temple in Jerusalem, which Cyrus had restored to them.

The leader of the expedition was Sheshbazzar, a prince of Judah, who may possibly have been one of the sons of the captive king Jehoiachin. Sheshbazzar appointed twelve men to help him, two of whom played a big part in the rebuilding of Jerusalem. The first was Zerubbabel, a member of the family of David; the second was Joshua (or Jeshua), the chief priest. The Bible says nothing of what happened on the long journey; but we can picture the joyful travellers, with their servants, their horses, mules, camels and asses, as they trekked day after day along the burning tracks of the desert. With them, we are told, went men and women singers; and every now and then the singers must have led the other travellers in a psalm of thankfulness and praise.

We learn what happened after the arrival in Jerusalem from the books of Ezra and Nehemiah. The people were absolutely overjoyed to be back; but there were many difficulties for them to face. Very little remained of the ancient kingdom of Judah—probably no more than an area of forty square miles round about Jerusalem. There were people living in the country, people from the surrounding tribes. They had drifted in after the Jews had been taken to Babylonia, and some of them had married into the families of the weakly, poverty-stricken Jews who had been left behind by Nebuchadnezzar. They had not tried to rebuild any of the cities which the Babylonians had destroyed, and Jerusalem was still a heap of ruins. All they had done was to build a few houses and cultivate a few patches of land; but the country itself was neglected and desolate.

The people of the north were known as Samaritans (after Samaria, the former kingdom of Israel). Like the people of Judah, they were of mixed descent; and they are called in the Bible "the adversaries of Judah and Benjamin". Some of them were friendly enough in the beginning, for they offered to help in rebuilding the Temple. But Zerubbabel, who was in charge of the rebuilding, and Joshua, the priest, refused their offer because they feared that if they accepted pagan customs would be introduced into the worship of God. "Ye have nothing to do with us to build an house unto our God," said Zerubbabel and Joshua; "but we ourselves together will build unto the Lord God of Israel, as king Cyrus the king of Persia hath commanded us."

The adversaries of Judah and Benjamin were so annoyed by this refusal that they did all they could to stir up trouble and to hinder the work. But, undeterred, the Jews cleared away the rubble from the ruined Temple, set up an altar, and laid the foundations of a new building. There was great rejoicing when this had been done; but then the work began to flag. In Babylonia the Jews had led well-ordered, comfortable lives; but now they had to put up with hardship and poverty. They longed above everything to complete the Temple; but progress was slow, and they were in daily danger from their enemies, particularly from the Edomites, who had settled in the country to the south of Jerusalem. The Jews were also in need of houses; and work on the Temple was held up while they made homes for themselves.

Two prophets encouraged the people to go on with their task of rebuilding the Temple. Their names were Haggai and Zechariah; and they began to preach in the year 520. They believed that once the Temple had been completed and its worship restored, the other kingdoms of the world would be overthrown by God, who would raise Jerusalem above all the nations. They thought, too, that a representative of God, the Messiah ("Messiah" means "anointed") would lead the people in righteousness; and they imagined that Zerubbabel would prove to be this Messiah. The books of Haggai and Zechariah are filled with details about the services and sacrifices which would be held in the new Temple; but Zechariah, whose book is much longer than Haggai's, made one of the great religious pronouncements in the Bible. The will of God is not carried out by force, he told Zerubbabel, who may well have been growing rather arrogant: "Not by might, nor by power, but by my spirit, saith the Lord of hosts."

In 515 B.C., five-and-a-half years after Haggai and Zechariah began to preach, the Temple was completed and solemnly dedicated. But the people who had laboured so hard to build it were living under conditions which were becoming more and more difficult. The land, which had been neglected for so long, did not produce enough food; and poverty was becoming widespread. Before very long Jerusalem, where rebuilding had been going on, fell into disrepair; and nobody seemed able to make a start on rebuilding the other towns and villages. As time went on, some of the Jews married foreigners who had settled in the country; and their children lacked their own strong faith.

In these dark and troubled years two new leaders came forward, Nehemiah and Ezra. Nehemiah held an important post at the Persian court, as cup-bearer to the king. Cyrus had been killed in battle in 530 B.C., and the present king was Artaxerxes I. Under Persian rule Judah (or Judea as it later came to be called) was a province of Persia, but it was allowed a great deal of independence.

Ezra, who was a priest and a scribe, travelled to Jerusalem from Babylon with a number of other priests. Scholars differ about the date of his arrival. Some of them think that it was in 457 B.C.; others that it was not until very much later. But, while Ezra's date is uncertain, we know that Nehemiah went to Jerusalem in 445. He had heard how badly his people were faring, and he felt that his place was with them. In the Bible he tells the story in his own words, how when he brought Artaxerxes his wine the king noticed that he was looking sad. "Now I had not been beforetime sad in his presence. Wherefore the king said unto me, Why is thy countenance sad, seeing thou art not sick? this is nothing else but sorrow of the heart. Then I was very sore afraid, And said unto the king, Let the king live for ever: why should not my countenance be sad, when the city, the place of my fathers' sepulchres, lieth waste, and the gates thereof are consumed with fire? Then the king said unto me, For what dost thou make request? So I prayed to the God of heaven. And I said unto the king, If it pleases the king, and if thy servant have found favour in thy sight, that thou wouldest send me unto Judah, unto the city of my fathers' sepulchres, that I may build it."

Artaxerxes not only granted Nehemiah a long leave of absence but appointed him governor of Judah, with authority to rule as he thought best. So Nehemiah went thankfully to Jerusalem where he spent many years. At the king's request he returned to Babylon for a short time in 432 B.C.; but there was still much to be done in Jerusalem, and the king let him go back.

Nehemiah started work three days after his arrival in Jerusalem by making a tour of the city wall. He found it as badly damaged as he had feared. He therefore called the priests, nobles and people together and addressed them. "Ye see," he said, "the distress that we are in, how Jerusalem lieth waste, and the gates thereof are burned with fire: come, and let us build up the wall of Jerusalem, that we be no more a reproach. . . . And they said, Let us rise up and build. So they strengthened their hands for this good work."

Repairs were carried out under great difficulty and daily threats of attack. Chief among Nehemiah's enemies was Sanballat, governor of Samaria. Sanballat and his friends, who were probably of mixed Israelite and Canaanite descent, at first offered to help; but, like Zerubbabel before him, Nehemiah refused to employ anybody who was not a Jew. After this they did everything they could to bring the work to a stop; but, despite their threats, it went on steadily. It is said that the men worked with a builder's tool in one hand and a sword in the other. Nehemiah himself was constantly on guard. He and his chief helpers scarcely slept; and he seemed to the builders to be everywhere at once, with his heartening rallying cry: "Our God will fight for us."

Nehemiah inspired his men to work as they had never worked before. He was a really great man, one of the truly great men in Bible history, a man of courage and resolution; and his influence over his fellow men came from his deep, unwavering faith in God.

Within a few weeks the wall had been completely repaired and lacked only its gates. Nehemiah then felt free to start making some very important reforms. Despite everything the prophets had said in the past, the poor were being most harshly oppressed by the rich nobles and officials. In times of drought and famine the poor were unable to pay their taxes; and so they had to barter their houses, vineyards and fields in exchange for money for their taxes and their food. When they could not repay the money they had borrowed they had to sell themselves or their children as slaves.

When the poor people realized that Nehemiah was a just governor they came to him to complain of their plight. "I was very angry when I heard their cry and these words," declared Nehemiah. "Then I consulted with myself, and I rebuked the nobles, and the rulers." Nehemiah made his charges in public, before the whole community. He and his helpers, he said, had been doing their utmost to buy back those Jews who had sold themselves as slaves to foreigners. But, he went on, his fellow-Jews had actually been selling their brothers into slavery just because they knew that he would buy them back. In this way, the rich men were getting their money at the expense of the poor and of the country's treasury.

When Nehemiah had finished speaking the accused men stood silent. They knew the charges against them were true.

"It is not good that ye do," said Nehemiah solemnly. "Ought ye not to walk in the fear of our God because of the reproach of the heathen our enemies?" He went on to tell them that while they had been growing rich he and his helpers had been lending money and grain to the poor without demanding any interest. He appealed to the nobles and officials to do the same; and he asked them to return to the poor all the property they had taken from them, together with one per cent—or one-hundredth part —of the money, grain, wine and oil which had been exacted as interest. The nobles and officials now saw how wrongly they had behaved. "We will restore them, and will require nothing of them," they promised. "So will we do as thou sayest."

Nehemiah was not at all sure that he could trust the nobles and officials to keep their word. So, in order to make their promise binding, he made them repeat it as an oath before the priests. After this he explained that although, as governor, he was empowered to levy a tax on the people for his own expenses, he had never done so. Instead, he used his own money to feed at his table those Jews and men from other tribes who came to visit him.

When Sanballat of Samaria and his friends learned that the wall was ready except for its gates they decided to get rid of the troublesome governor. They invited him to a conference outside the city; but he refused, for he suspected that they were trying to lure him into a trap. "I am doing a great work, so that I cannot come down," he told them. "Why should the work cease, whilst I leave it, and come down to you?"

Four times Sanballat repeated his request, but each time Nehemiah refused. Then Sanballat tried other tactics. He sent him a letter saying that he had heard a rumour that Nehemiah was planning to make himself king and had actually asked certain prophets to speak of him as king. If Artaxerxes heard this report, Sanballat added, he would be extremely angry; and he urged Nehemiah to come out and discuss it. Once again Nehemiah refused. The charge, he declared, was absolutely false.

Sanballat made one more attempt to trap Nehemiah. He bribed some of the prophets to frighten him with a prophecy that he was about to be killed; and one of the prophets went to the governor and begged him to take shelter in the Temple. Even though Nehemiah seems to have thought that the prophet was sincere he refused to show any sign of fear in front of the people. "Should such a man as I flee?" he demanded. "And who is there, that, being as I am, would go into the temple to save his life? I will not go in."

There was nothing further Sanballat could do. He had to stand by while the gates of Jerusalem were set up, and the whole work was dedicated to God. The task of rebuilding had been carried out in the incredibly short space of fifty-two days.

During the years he spent in Jerusalem Nehemiah made a number of religious reforms. He was utterly determined to keep the religious life of the Jews strong and lasting. He was sure that he could not do this if they continued to marry foreigners; for he feared that they would bring up their children without their own faith. He therefore did everything he could to prevent foreign marriages; and, when he discovered that a priest had married one of Sanballat's daughters, he expelled the man from serving in the Temple, as an example to the others. He also arranged for the priests to hold daily worship in the Temple; and he insisted that all the people should observe the Sabbath strictly, and pay taxes for the upkeep of the Temple.

Nehemiah was a stern man as well as a brave one. But he was completely honest and unselfish in his dealings with others; and the people's readiness to obey him shows how much they admired and respected him.

Ezra, the other great reformer, was also strong and stern. According to the Bible, he and Nehemiah were in Jerusalem at the same time; but many scholars today think he reached Jerusalem in 397 B.C., nearly fifty years after Nehemiah, and that by that time some of Nehemiah's reforms had been allowed to lapse.

The two men were very much alike. They both had intense faith in God. Both were leaders of men, hardworking and full of courage; and both were ruthless in their determination to stop foreign marriages. But, while Nehemiah was a practical man and, as governor, could order things to be done, Ezra was a priest, and his special task was to teach. He took with him to Jerusalem a company of about 5,000, including a large number of priests, and many gifts from the Persian king. The journey took four months and it passed without incident. "The hand of our God was upon us," said Ezra, "and he delivered us from the hand of the enemy and of such as lay in wait by the way."

The arrival in Jerusalem of Ezra and his followers was most timely. Judah was still poverty stricken and short of people. The newcomers were ready to work hard for their religion and their country, and they brought useful gifts with them.

The most precious gift they brought was a book of the Law of Moses. When the people of Jerusalem learned that Ezra had the book with him they implored him to show it to them. And so, in the presence of a vast crowd of men, women and children who had assembled in a wide space in front of the water-gate on the east of the city, Ezra mounted a wooden pulpit and held the book high for all to see. Then he "blessed the Lord, the great God. And all the people answered, Amen, Amen, with lifting up their hands: and they bowed their heads, and worshipped the Lord with their faces to the ground."

On that day and on every other day Ezra read aloud to the assembled company a portion of the book of the Law; and after each reading the meaning of the words was carefully explained. On the first day Ezra must have read passages which reminded the people of their faults and failings; for, "all the people wept when they heard the words of the law". Ezra meant them to repent; and he set aside a day on which they had to fast, wear sackcloth, and confess their sins. But he also wanted them to learn that happiness came from obedience to the Law; and so he told them that on the first day they should not grieve. "This day is holy unto our Lord: neither be ye sorry; for the joy of the Lord is your strength."

Ezra then ordered the people to go up into the hills and gather branches of olive, myrtle, palm and other leafy trees. With these they made booths and lived in them for seven days while they celebrated the festival of Tabernacles—the harvest festival—with thanksgiving and rejoicing.

In some ways, however, Ezra was a much sterner man than Nehemiah. When he saw that foreign marriages were weakening the unity of the Jews, he issued an edict ordering every man who had married a foreigner to leave his wife. This edict must have brought unhappiness and hardship to many wives and children. The Bible does not say if anything was done to help them; but, although Ezra was harsh he was not cruel, and we can imagine that he did what he could to relieve their sufferings. Many scholars think that the story of Ruth (we shall read about it in the last chapter of this book) was written about this time as a protest against Ezra's edict. Ruth was a foreigner—a Moabitess—who married a Jew and accepted his faith; and from this marriage between a Jew and a foreigner, we are told, sprang David, the greatest of Israel's kings, who was Ruth's grandson.

But, if Nehemiah and Ezra were stern, between them they welded the people into a united community, united in faith and in obedience to the Law. With this unity came strength and prosperity, and peace which lasted for many years to come.

Three prophets—Obadiah, Joel and Malachi—lived round about this time. The book of Obadiah consists of a single short chapter attacking the Edomites, who had taken advantage of Judah's weakness during the exile to settle in the country to the south of Jerusalem. Scholars still disagree about the dates of the prophet Joel. His book (it has only three chapters) describes drought, famine and other disasters as God's judgment on the people for their wrongdoing. But, adds Joel, God is just. He will have mercy on the stricken people and revive them. "And ye shall know that I am in the midst of Israel, and that I am the Lord your God, and none else: and my people shall never be ashamed."

The book of Malachi is the last of the books of the Hebrew prophets. Malachi may not have been the prophet's name, for it simply means in Hebrew, "my messenger"; and it occurs in the first sentence of the book: "The burden of the word of the Lord to Israel by Malachi." The prophet's name does not matter: it is his message that is important. Malachi pleaded for friendship and brotherhood between the peoples of all races. He longed for all those who believed in God to become part of the family of Israel; and it may be that he disliked the harsh measures taken by Nehemiah and Ezra to prevent outsiders from building the Temple and Jews from marrying foreigners. "Have we not all one father?" asked Malachi. "Hath not one God created us? Why do we deal treacherously every man against his brother, by profaning the covenant of our fathers?"

The last ten chapters of the book of Isaiah probably belong to the same period. The name (or names) of the author is unknown; and so he has been called Trito-Isaiah, or the Third Isaiah.

The Third Isaiah criticised and denounced the people for their sins and their empty worship; but his message was also full of hope and confidence:

"And shall say, Cast ye up, cast ye up, prepare the way, take up the stumblingblock out of the way of my people.

"For thus saith the high and lofty One that inhabiteth eternity, whose name is Holy; I dwell in the high and holy place, with him also that is of a contrite and humble spirit, to revive the spirit of the humble, and to revive the heart of the contrite ones."

Like Malachi, the Third Isaiah believed in the brotherhood of man, and wanted the peoples of other nations to join the religious community of Israel:

"Also the sons of the stranger, that join themselves to the Lord, to serve him, and to love the name of the Lord, to be his servants, every one that keepeth the sabbath from polluting it, and taketh hold of my covenant;

"Even them will I bring to my holy mountain, and make them joyful in my house of prayer . . . for mine house shall be called an house of prayer for all people . . ."

CHAPTER XIV

POEMS AND LEGENDS

THE BIBLE HISTORY of the Jews ends with the books of
Nehemiah and Ezra; but, of course, their history went on. Other
books are included in the Hebrew Bible but they are not history.
Some are poems or legends which were included because they
had a message; and several of the most famous of them are
grouped together in this chapter.

Somewhere about the time of Nehemiah and Ezra an unknown
Jew (or Jews) wrote a book which is both a story and a poem.
This is the book of Job. It deals with a problem which the author
could not solve—and which has not yet been solved. It is the
problem of why innocent people should suffer.

The author describes Job as a wise, upright and very religious
man, who is happy in his life and his family. And God—so the
story goes—decides to test Job's faith by overwhelming him with
disaster. Job loses every single thing he prizes, his family, his
possessions, and his health. In ancient times, as we saw, people
thought that all disasters came as a punishment for sin. The author
of the book of Job did not believe this, because he describes Job
as an ideal man, who has done no wrong at all but who suffers

just the same. But Job's friends, who come to try to comfort him in his loss, are sure he must have committed some very grave crimes, and they implore him to repent.

The first part of the book is written in prose; but at this point it turns into poetry—or rather into a poetic play. It is in the form of an argument between Job and his friends, who refuse to believe in his innocence. Job agrees that if a man suffers then he must have sinned; but he has not done wrong, he tells them, and he is hurt because they will not believe him and so cannot console him. But far worse than this is the feeling that he has been treated unjustly; and in his pain and distress he cries out to all-powerful God. God, he cries, is his judge and his champion, and in God is his hope.

In the poem God Himself talks with Job. First He rebukes him for his doubts and his ignorance; and in this passage the writer makes it clear that God, creator of the world, is so great that we cannot understand Him. "Where wast thou," God demands, "when I laid the foundations of the earth? declare, if thou hast understanding." God asks Job many other questions which he cannot answer; but then he speaks to him as a comforter and friend. And to Job, the feeling that God is near is all that matters. The disasters which have befallen him no longer count.

The last chapter of the book is in prose, like the beginning. It tells how Job's faith and his patience are rewarded; for he is cured of an illness, he marries again, and his prosperity is restored. The story of Job is a splendid one; for, although Job cannot understand why he has been made to suffer, he is content to leave the answer to the wisdom of God. And the book of Job contains some of the wisest and most beautiful passages in the Bible. In one passage Job speaks of the comparative worthlessness of the valuable things produced in the earth, the gold, silver and jewels. Then he asks:

"But where shall wisdom be found? and where is the place of understanding?

Man knoweth not the price thereof; neither is it found in the land of the living.

The depth saith, It is not in me: and the sea saith, It is not with me.

It cannot be gotten for gold, neither shall silver be weighed for the price thereof.

It cannot be valued with the gold of Ophir, with the precious onyx, or the sapphire.

The gold and the crystal cannot equal it: and the exchange of it shall not be for jewels of fine gold.

No mention shall be made of coral, or of pearls: for the price of wisdom is above rubies. . . .

Whence then cometh wisdom? and where is the place of understanding? . . .

God understandeth the way thereof, and he knoweth the place thereof.

For he looketh to the ends of the earth, and seeth under the whole heaven;

To make the weight for the winds; and he weigheth the waters by measure.

When he made a decree for the rain, and a way for the lightning of the thunder:

Then did he see it, and declare it; he prepared it, yea, and searched it out.

And unto man he said, Behold, the fear of the Lord, that is wisdom; and to depart from evil is understanding."

The finest passage in the book of Job is his great declaration of faith:

"Oh that my words were now written! oh that they were printed in a book!

That they were graven with an iron pen and lead in the rock for ever!

For I know that my redeemer liveth, and that he shall stand
at the latter day upon the earth:

And though after my skin worms destroy this body, yet in
my flesh shall I see God:

When I shall see for myself, and mine eyes shall behold, and
not another."

This passage needs explaining. In ancient times when a man was
in trouble it was the duty of his nearest relative to help—or
vindicate him. The relative was called a redeemer—or vindicator;
but Job sees his redeemer not as a man but as God Himself. Some
scholars think that in this passage Job is speaking of an event
which will happen in his lifetime: others, that it will take place
only after his death. To many Christians—though not to Jews—
the redeemer is Jesus, although the book of Job was written
centuries before he died. The passage, then, means different
things to different people; but to all of us it is a fine message of
faith in God.

The book of Daniel, generally thought to be a very late book,
dating from about 166 B.C., was written to hearten the Jews
during a period of trouble. By this time there had been many
changes in their lives. Between 333 and 331 B.C. Alexander the
Great, the brilliant young Greek king of Macedon, had overthrown the king of Persia, captured all the cities along the coast
of the Mediterranean, and conquered Egypt. Alexander was still
very young when he died; and after his death his vast empire,
which included Judah, was divided. But Alexander's influence—
the influence of Greek worship and customs—remained very
strong. Although the Jews did not worship the Greek gods some
of them adopted the Greek way of life. A number of them left
Judah altogether. Others stayed on, faithful to their own religion
and laws. The Jews in Judah no longer had a king, and they were
not a nation. Their leader was the high priest, who was anointed
with oil, as the kings of old had been.

For more than a hundred years the nations quarrelled over the ownership of Judah. Then it fell to Syria. In the year 168 B.C. Antiochus IV, the king of Syria, made up his mind to destroy the independent spirit of the Jews, stamp out their religion, and force them to worship the Greek gods. He sent an army to attack Jerusalem; and his soldiers slew many of the people and sacked the Temple. Antiochus then issued a decree forbidding the surviving Jews to worship God on pain of death.

In the years which followed a courageous band of pious Jews, led by members of the Hasmonaean family (or Maccabees, as they are often called) defied Antiochus, harried his troops, and rededicated the Temple. Their history is not told in the Bible but in the Apocrypha,—a later collection of religious and historical writings—and so it does not belong here.*

The book of Daniel was possibly written about two years after the forces of Antiochus had sacked Jerusalem, at a time when those Jews who clung to their religion were most in need of encouragement. The hero of the story is a Jew, the just and wise statesman Daniel. And the object of the book was to show that if Daniel and other brave Jews could resist persecution, so, too, could the pious Jews of Judah. Their sufferings, said the author, were small in comparison with the sufferings of their ancestors. He therefore told them a story, which he set in the reign of Nebuchadnezzar, about three Jews, Shadrach, Meshach and Abednego, who refused to obey an order given by the king that they should bow down and worship a golden idol. As a punishment Nebuchadnezzar had them bound and flung alive into a burning furnace, which was so fierce that their captors were burned when they opened the furnace doors. The three pious Jews came to no harm; and it was reported to Nebuchadnezzar that they were walking about in the furnace and that with them was another figure—an angel. "Then Nebuchadnezzar came near to the mouth of the burning fiery furnace, and spake, and said, Shadrach, Meshach, and Abednego,

* It is described in *Leaders of the People* by Josephine Kamm (Abelard-Schumann), pp. 40-51.

ye servants of the most high God, come forth, and come hither!"
When the Jews approached him Nebuchadnezzar gave orders
that they and their people should be allowed to worship as they
chose, and he blessed their God.

The meaning of this story is that although Nebuchadnezzar
was a far more powerful king than Antiochus, neither he nor the
tyrant Antiochus was anything in comparison with God, who
could work such a miracle on behalf of those men who were
faithful in their worship.

Among the other stories in the book is the story of Belshazzar's
feast, of which we heard earlier. At this feast Daniel was the man
who was able to translate the mysterious writing which had
appeared on the wall. In yet another story (the author sets it in
the time of Darius the Great who came to the throne of Babylonia
forty years after the death of Nebuchadnezzar) Daniel, the king's
most respected adviser, is again the hero. When he refuses to obey
an edict that Darius should be worshipped as a god, he is flung
into a den of savage lions. Daniel, like Shadrach, Meshach and
Abednego, is saved from a cruel death by an angel; and Darius,
like Nebuchadnezzar before him, blesses the living God.

The idea which inspired the book of Daniel was the greatness of
God and the smallness of man. Even a man as just and wise as
Daniel would have achieved nothing without the spirit of God
working within him. The book was written with a special purpose; and, perhaps because the author wanted to comfort his
people, he predicted within a certain space of time the death of
the tyrant Antiochus, the deliverance of the Jews, and the beginning of a new and better age in history.

This must have heartened the tried and persecuted Jews and
helped them to resist.

The book of Daniel also contains a passage which refers to
resurrection—or revival—after death. "And many of them that
sleep in the dust of the earth shall awake, some to everlasting life,
and some to shame and everlasting contempt. And they that be
wise shall shine as the brightness of the firmament; and they that

turn many to righteousness as the stars for ever and ever." In the Psalms there are some early passages which possibly refer to life after death; but the most famous passage occurs in the Apocrypha, in the section called the Wisdom of Solomon. "The souls of the righteous are in the hand of God, and no evil shall touch them. In the eyes of the simple they seem to have died, and their departure is accounted to be their hurt. But they are in peace, and their hope is full of immortality. Having borne a little chastening, they shall receive great good; for God has made trial of them, and found them worthy of himself."

One of the loveliest and most moving of all the Bible stories is the legend of Ruth. It is set in the time of the Judges, but, as we saw, it was probably written hundreds of years later.

Ruth, we are told, was not a Hebrew. She belonged to the tribe of Moabites, and she had married a Hebrew whose family had settled in Moab. The family consisted of Ruth's husband, his brother, and their parents. One by one the men of the family died, leaving only the women—Ruth, her sister-in-law, Orpah, and Naomi, her mother-in-law.

Naomi decided to return to Judah, to her own people. She said farewell to her daughters-in-law, blessed them, and told them that she hoped they would marry again. Orpah remained in Moab, but Ruth, who loved her mother-in-law dearly, refused to leave her. "Intreat me not to leave thee," she said, "or to return from following after thee: for whither thou goest, I will go; and where thou lodgest, I will lodge; thy people shall be my people, and thy God my God: Where thou diest, will I die, and there will I be buried: the Lord do so to me, and more also, if ought but death part thee and me." And when Naomi saw that Ruth was determined to accompany her she said no more to prevent her.

The story goes on to tell how the kind and gentle Ruth finds a new husband, a kinsman of Naomi's husband, and of how they settle in the village of Bethlehem. Ruth's second husband is Boaz, a good man and a landowner, who first sees Ruth working in his fields with the other women. Ruth and Boaz have a son; and his birth is a great joy to them and to Naomi, who had no grandchildren of her own. And this child—so the story ends—became the grandfather of David.

The purpose of the story of Ruth is to show that God is the God of all peoples, not simply the God of the Hebrews. Ruth, a foreigner, joins the family of Israel and becomes the ancestress of David, the greatest of Israel's kings.

The legend of Esther is about a heroic Hebrew woman who marries a Persian king. There is absolutely no proof that Esther ever existed, but the king was a real man. He was Ahasuerus (or Xerxes) who reigned from 486 to 465 B.C. The story of Esther is one of hatred and strife. It is an exciting story, but it does not show religious teaching at its best.

Ahasuerus, we are told, was married to another woman, Vashti; but we have no proof of Vashti's existence either. Vashti had apparently offended the king by refusing to appear before him when he was feasting with his nobles; and, since disobedience to the king was a crime, he divorced her. He then sent messengers all over the kingdom to find beautiful women from whom he might choose himself a new wife.

Among the other women brought to court by the king's messengers was Esther, an orphan, who had been brought up by her uncle, a pious Jew named Mordecai. When the king saw Esther he fell in love with her, and married her. He did not know at first that she was a Jewess, for her uncle had advised her to say nothing about it.

Now the king had appointed a viceroy called Haman, and had ordered everybody to pay homage to him. Mordecai, who would pay homage only to God, refused to bow down to Haman; and this made Haman so angry that he persuaded the king that his Hebrew subjects were plotting to murder him. Ahasuerus believed Haman's tale and gave orders that on a certain day the Jews throughout his kingdom should be killed. When Mordecai heard of the decree he sent a message to Esther telling her to go to the king and plead for the lives of her people. This was a dangerous task; for no one—not even the queen—might enter the king's presence uninvited, on pain of death if he was displeased. But Esther was a brave woman. She sent back a message to her uncle asking him to gather the Jews together and to hold a fast. "I also and my maidens will fast likewise;" she said. "And so will I go in unto the king, which is not according to the law: and if I perish, I perish."

The king loved his wife so dearly that when he saw her and realised she had a request to make, he told her that he would give her anything she wanted. Esther replied that she would make her request if the king and Haman would honour her by attending a banquet with her the next day. Haman was very flattered by the invitation; but his pleasure was spoilt by the sight of Mordecai, who stood outside the palace gates and refused to pay homage to him as he passed.

Haman then ordered his servants to put up some gallows; and he went to the king to ask permission for Mordecai to be hanged. Unluckily for Haman, Ahasuerus had spent part of the night listening to a reading of the chronicles of his reign. He had learned from the chronicles that Mordecai had once uncovered a plot to kill him, but had received no reward.

Before Haman had had time to make his request the king asked him a question: "What shall be done unto the man whom the king delighteth to honour?" Haman imagined that the king was referring to him; and so he suggested that the man should be clad in the king's own robes and crown and seated on the king's own horse; and that one of the princes should lead him into the city, proclaiming that here was the man the king delighted to honour. This seemed an excellent idea to Ahasuerus. He ordered Haman to carry it out with Mordecai as the hero; and Haman dared not refuse.

Esther's banquet for the king and Haman lasted for two days. On the second day the king asked her to name her request.

Esther first denounced Haman for his plot to kill Mordecai and his wicked lie about her people; and then implored him to spare her people's lives. The king, shocked by Haman's wicked cruelty, gave orders for him to be hanged from the gallows he had prepared for Mordecai; and he made Mordecai viceroy in Haman's place. He also revoked the decree ordering the massacre of the Jews; and let it be known that throughout his kingdom the Jews had his permission to slay their enemies.

The story of Esther, like the story of Daniel, must have been written to hearten the Jews during a time of persecution. It is a very vivid story; and it shows clearly that persecution is an evil thing, and that it brings out a vengeful spirit in the persecuted.

The legend of Jonah is told as a sermon. Jonah, a prophet, has been ordered by God to go to Nineveh, the capital of Assyria. When he gets there he is to tell the people that because of their many sins their city is to be destroyed. But Jonah is afraid to undertake this mission; and he secretly boards a ship going in the opposite direction. While the ship is at sea a violent storm arises and the sailors fear the ship will be wrecked and they will be drowned. They are very superstitious and think that someone on board must have brought them ill luck. They draw lots to find out the bringer of misfortune, and declare him to be Jonah. Jonah tells the sailors that he is fleeing from the duty imposed on him by God and deserves to be punished. "Take me up, and cast me forth into the sea," he says, "so shall the sea be calm unto you: for I know that for my sake this great tempest is upon you."

The sailors do as Jonah tell them, and immediately the sea calms down. Jonah himself is not drowned. Instead, he is swallowed by an enormous fish which, three days later, casts him safe and un-injured on to dry land.

When Jonah again hears God's command to preach in Nineveh he hastens to obey. As the Ninevites listen to his preaching they repent sincerely of their sins; and God tells Jonah that because the people have repented He will pardon them and their city will be

spared. Instead of pleasing Jonah this makes him angry. He feels
that he has been made to look a fool by prophesying something
which does not take place. He is so angry that he sits down in the
burning sun outside the city walls and asks God to allow him to
die. As he sits waiting for something to happen a quick-growing
plant springs up and gives him some very welcome shade. But
the plant withers as quickly as it grew; and Jonah is even more
angry than he was before. "And God said to Jonah, Doest thou
well to be angry for the gourd? And he said, I do well to be angry,
even unto death. Then said the Lord, Thou hast had pity on the
gourd, for the which thou hast not laboured, neither madest it
grow; which came up in a night, and perished in a night: And
should not I spare Nineveh, that great city, wherein are more than
sixscore thousand* persons that cannot discern between their
right hand and their left hand; and also much cattle?"

God's rebuke to Jonah repeats several lessons which the Jews
are taught elsewhere in the Bible. One is that God is the God of all
peoples, the pagan people of Nineveh as well as of the Jews.
Another is that if people are truly repentant, then punishment
may be averted. And a third lesson is that children who have not
yet learned the difference between right and wrong ("persons
that cannot discern between their right hand and their left hand")
and dumb animals shall not be made to suffer for the sins of
their elders.

The stories in this chapter may be interesting in themselves;
but today most people find them much less interesting than
stories of events which actually took place. Historians and
archaeologists are constantly making new discoveries about Bible
history. Perhaps the most exciting discovery of them all was
made in 1947. In that year the famous Dead Sea Scrolls were
found hidden in a cave on the western shore of the Dead Sea, just
south of Jericho. Among these scrolls were two on which the
book of Isaiah had been written, which proved to be about a

* 120,000.

thousand years older than the text used in the Bible. Another was an explanation of the first two chapters of the book of Habbakuk. These scrolls are making it possible for scholars to compare the ancient text with later texts, and to make important discoveries about language. Other scrolls, which were written about two thousand years ago, are helping scholars to find out more about life in Palestine.

So the search goes on. And the most fascinating thing about it is that so often, as we have seen, the discoveries made in modern times prove that the story recorded in the Bible is true history. Even more important, we have in the Bible the great religious and moral book of mankind.